KET
Practice
Tests ▶ Plus

Peter Lucantoni

Longman

Contents

Exam Overview

PAPER 1 Reading and Writing
(1 hour 10 minutes)

Part 1 – Signs

For questions 1–5 you match five signs to the correct explanation A, B or C.

For questions 6–10 you match eight signs with five explanations.

Part 2 – Definitions

For questions 11–15 you match a group of eight topic-related words with five definitions.

Part 3 – Everyday conversations

For questions 16–20 you complete five two-line conversations by choosing A, B or C.

For questions 21–25 you complete a longer conversation. You choose from a list of options. There are five spaces and eight options.

Part 4 – Factual text

For questions 26–32 you answer seven questions about a short text. You have to choose the right answer A, B or C.

Part 5 – Factual text

For questions 33–40 you read a short factual text with eight numbered spaces. You choose one word A, B or C to fill each space.

Part 6 – Notes, short message, letter

For questions 41–50 you read a short text with ten numbered spaces. The text is a short letter or note. You have to think of one word for each space.

Part 7 – Form completion

For questions 51–55 you read a short text and then you complete a form using information from the text (words and short phrases only).

Part 8 – Continuous writing

For question 56 you write a short note or message to someone (20–25 words).

PAPER 2 Listening
(about 25 minutes)

Part 1 – Five short dialogues

For questions 1–5 you listen to five short conversations and you choose the correct picture A, B or C.

Part 2 – Conversation

For questions 6–10 you listen to a conversation between two people. You match five questions in two lists.

Part 3 – Conversation

For questions 11–15 you listen to a conversation between two people and answer five questions by choosing A, B or C.

Part 4 – Conversation

For questions 16–20 you listen to a conversation and write down missing information in messages or notes. You write one or two words or numbers.

Part 5 – Factual monologue

For questions 21–25 you listen to a monologue and write down missing information in a message or notes.

You write one or two words or numbers. The monologue is often a recorded telephone message.

PAPER 3 Speaking
(8–10 minutes)

Part 1 – Personal information

You give personal, factual information about yourself (family and friends, job or studies, daily life, interests and likes). You will probably be with another student. One examiner asks you some questions. The other listens. This part lasts 5–6 minutes.

Part 2 – Prompt card activity

You have to make five questions and ask your partner. Then you have to answer your partner's questions. The examiner will just listen to you. The questions will be about personal or non-personal information. This part lasts 3–4 minutes.

TEST 1

PAPER 1   Reading and Writing   (1 hour 10 minutes)

PREPARATION

Part 1 – signs

- For **questions 1 – 5**, you read signs and notices which you might see in shops, railway or bus stations, airports, schools, restaurants, sports clubs, etc.
- The questions ask:
  Where can you see these notices?   OR   Who are these notices for?
- You choose the correct answer **A**, **B** or **C**.

1 ⟩ **Read the instructions to the exam task opposite.**

1   What question do you have to answer?
2   Where do you mark your answers in the exam?

2 ⟩ **Look at the example 0. Why is C the right answer?**

1   Where can you find animals?
2   Can you find animals in a station or a café?

3 ⟩ **Vocabulary focus: places**

For this part you need to know words for places, and what you can do there.

a ⟩ **Match the places with the actions. Some actions match with more than one place.**

1	newsagent's	a)	buy a book
2	bookshop	b)	go fishing
3	restaurant	c)	buy fruit
4	supermarket	d)	eat a meal
5	library	e)	play basketball
6	market	f)	go shopping
7	disco	g)	go swimming
8	beach	h)	dance
9	sports centre	i)	look for some information
10	river	j)	buy a newspaper

b ⟩ **Say what you can do or buy in each place.**

Examples: You can buy a newspaper at the newsagent's.
              You can buy a book in a bookshop.

c ⟩ **Make a list of other places you know.**

Examples: café, cinema

d ⟩ **Say what you can do or buy in each place.**

Examples: You can drink coffee in a café.
              You can see a film at the cinema.

4 ⟩ **Do the exam task. Use the clues to help you.**

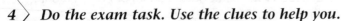

Part 1
Questions 1 – 5

Where can you see these notices?
For questions 1 – 5, mark A, B or C on the answer sheet.

EXAMPLE		ANSWER
0 **PLEASE DO NOT FEED THE ANIMALS**	A in a station B in a café C in a zoo	C

1 **We take newspapers to your home!**

    A at a newsagent's
    B in a taxi office
    C in a bookshop

2 *Oranges 80p per kilo*

    A in a restaurant
    B in a supermarket
    C in a café

3 **At busy times, customers can only swim for one hour**

    A in a disco
    B on the beach
    C at a sports centre

4 *Return books here – 10p per day if late*

    A in a library
    B in a hotel
    C in a supermarket

5 **NO FISHING –** October to March

    A in a café
    B at a market
    C by a river

CLUES

Question 1: Where can you buy newspapers?

Question 2: You can find oranges in all three places but **where** can you *buy* them?

Question 3: You can swim at a sports centre and on the beach but **where** are you a *customer*?

Question 4: Where do you have to *return books*?

Question 5: You can find fish in all three places but **where** can you *go fishing*?

Part 1 – signs

- For **questions 6 – 10**, you read signs and notices which you might see in shops, railway or bus stations, airports, schools, restaurants, sports clubs, etc.
- You match each sign to the correct explanation.
- There are five explanations, but eight signs.

1 ⟩ Read the instructions to the exam task opposite.

1 What question do you have to answer?
2 How many questions are there?
3 Where do you mark your answers in the exam?

2 ⟩ Look at the example 0. Why is H the right answer?

1 <u>Underline</u> the words in the explanation that mean the same as No Smoking.
2 ⟨Circle⟩ the word that means Area.

3 ⟩ Grammar focus: can/can't, must/mustn't

The verbs *can/can't (cannot)*, *must/mustn't (must not)* often appear in explanations about signs.

Examples:
CASH ONLY = You **must** pay with cash. You **can't** pay by cheque.
NO ENTRY! DANGER! = You **mustn't** go in.

a ⟩ Complete the second sentence so that it means the same as the first. Use can't or must.

1 It is impossible to buy a ticket for the match.   You .... buy a ticket for the match.
2 It is very important to speak English in the classroom.   You .... speak English in the classroom.
3 It is not possible to swim in the pool today.   You .... swim in the pool today.
4 It is necessary to do your homework every day.   You .... do your homework every day.
5 Students have to pay at the end of each month.   You .... pay at the end of each month.

b ⟩ Look at the signs and complete the sentences using can/can't, must/mustn't.

1	ROAD CLOSED	You .... drive this way.
2	SHOP OPEN MONDAY – SATURDAY	You .... shop here every day except Sunday.
3	DANGER! ACCIDENT!	You .... drive carefully.
4	NO ENTRY	You .... go in this way.
5	TAXIS 24 HOURS A DAY	You .... get a taxi at any time.
6	PLEASE DO NOT WALK ON THE GRASS	You .... walk on the grass.
7	CONCERT IN THE PARK	You .... listen to music outside.
8	NO BOATS TO ISLAND	You .... travel today.
9	NO VISITORS AFTER 9 P.M.	Visitors .... leave by nine o'clock.
10	BOIL IN WATER FOR 20 MINUTES	You .... cook this before you eat it.

4 ⟩ Do the exam task. Use the clues to help you.

Part 1

Questions 6 – 10

Which notice (A – H) says this (6 – 10)?
For questions 6 – 10, mark the correct letter A – H on the answer sheet.

EXAMPLE	ANSWER
0 You can't smoke here.	**H**

6 You can buy food here.

7 You cannot go out this way.

8 You must take your medicine every day.

9 You mustn't cross the road here.

10 You can see live animals here.

A TWO TABLETS DAILY, AFTER EATING

B Busy traffic – Use bridge to cross

C All animal books half price

D FRUIT, VEGETABLE AND MEAT MARKET

E Hospital 500km ▶

F ZOO OPEN EVERY DAY 8 a.m. – 6 p.m.

G This door is locked Please use main exit

H No Smoking Area

CLUES

Question 6: Which sign mentions types of food?

Question 7: Why can't you go out this way? Which sign gives a reason?

Question 8: What kinds of medicine can you think of? Which sign mentions a type of medicine?

Question 9: Why mustn't you cross the road? How can you cross?

Question 10: Where can you see live (living) animals?

Part 2 – definitions

■ For **questions 11–15**, you match a group of words with the correct definition.

■ The words are related to one topic.

■ This part tests your vocabulary.

1 〉 *Vocabulary focus:* word sets

The following topics may be tested in the exam: food and drink, travel and transport, clothes, family relations, places, holidays, things in the house, etc.

a 〉 *Put the words in the box into the right group. Can you add any more?*

sandwich ~~blouse~~ platform butter jacket cheese journey chips skirt soup bus stop fish ticket sweater luggage boots

Food and drink	Travel and transport	Clothes
		blouse

b 〉 *Read the text and complete the chart.*

The Smith family

Tony is Mary's husband. They have two sons called Ben and Simon. Ben is married and his wife's name is Josie. Simon is single. Ben and Josie have three children, two sons and a daughter. James and his brother Ian are thirteen and fourteen years old. Their sister, whose name is Megan, is sixteen. They often go to visit their grandparents at weekends. Tony and Mary enjoy seeing their grandchildren.

The Smith family

Tony and (a) ....

(b) .... = (c) ....   (d) ....

(e) ....   (f) ....   (g) ....

2 〉 *Match the definitions with words from exercise 1.*

1   This is where you get on and off a train.   ....

2   You need these if you go walking in the mountains.   ....

3   You carry things in this when you go on a journey.   ....

4   These are the parents of your mother and father.   ....

5   You make this with two pieces of bread with cheese, meat, etc. between them.   ....

3 〉 *Ask and answer the questions.*

1   What's your favourite food?

2   How do you usually travel to school?

3   What do you like wearing best?

4   Describe your family.

4 〉 *Read the instructions to the exam task opposite.*

1   What vocabulary topic are all the words from?

2   How many questions are there?

3   Where do you mark your answers in the exam?

5 〉 *Look at the example 0. Why is A the right answer?*

There are many things to read in a library. What can you find a lot of?

6 〉 *Do the exam task. Use the clues to help you.*

Part 2

Questions 11–15

Read the descriptions (11–15) of some things you can read.
What is the correct word (A–H) for each description?
For questions 11–15, mark the correct letter A–H on the answer sheet.

EXAMPLE	ANSWER
0 There are many of these in a library.	**A**

11	This helps you to understand new words.	**A** book
		B comic
12	You need a computer to read this.	**C** dictionary
13	If you want to know when the bus arrives, you need this.	**D** email
		E magazine
14	Children enjoy the cartoons in this.	**F** newspaper
15	People often send one of these when they are on holiday.	**G** postcard
		H timetable

CLUES

Question 11: Where do you look if you don't know the meaning of a word?

Question 12: Which **one** item in the list needs a computer to read it?

Question 13: Where can you find information about the arrival of buses?

Question 14: Where do children usually read cartoons?

Question 15: What do people buy and send when they are on holiday?

Part 3 – everyday conversations

- For **questions 16 – 20**, you complete two-line conversations by choosing **A**, **B** or **C**.
- The conversations are often a question and an answer.

1 *Read the instructions to the exam task opposite.*

1 How many conversations are there?
2 Where do you mark your answers in the exam?

2 *Look at the example 0. Why is A the right answer?*

1 What is the question?
2 When we ask *where* someone comes from, the answer is always a country or a town, so the right answer is **A**. Why are **B** and **C** not possible?

3 *Grammar focus:* question words/tenses

To find the answer that matches the question, you need to look carefully at the question word (e.g. *Why? Where? Who?*), and the tense of the verb in the question.

a *Fill the spaces with the right question word.*

1	.... do you go to bed at night?	At 9.30.
2	.... do you live?	Near the town centre.
3	.... do you eat for breakfast?	Bread and butter.
4	.... is that over there?	My sister.
5	.... weren't you at school today?	Because I was ill.
6	.... students are there in your class?	Twenty.

b *Match the questions and the answers.*

1 <u>Did</u> you have a good time at the party?   a) Yes, she does.
2 <u>Does</u> your mother like her job?   b) Yes, I am.
3 Where <u>did</u> you go on holiday?   c) No, I don't.
4 <u>Are</u> you going to the match tonight?   d) Yes, I would.
5 <u>Do</u> you like Chinese food?   e) I went to Sicily.
6 <u>Would</u> you like to visit London?   f) No, I didn't.

4 *Can you complete each conversation?*

1 A: Do you speak English?   B: ....
2 A: Are you cold?   B: ....
3 A: Hello! How are you?   B: ....
4 A: Would you like an ice cream?   B: ....
5 A: When does the film start?   B: ....
6 A: Shall I turn on the TV?   B: ....

5 *Do the exam task. Use the clues to help you.*

Part 3
Questions 16 – 20

Complete the five conversations.
For questions 16 – 20, mark A, B or C on the answer sheet.

EXAMPLE		ANSWER
0	Where do you come from? **A** New York. **B** School. **C** Home.	**A**

16 What did you eat for dinner?

    A No, we didn't.
    B Spaghetti and salad.
    C We went to a restaurant.

17 Where did you put my CD player?

    A Yesterday.
    B Because it was broken.
    C On the bed.

18 Who did you see yesterday?

    A At the match.
    B My sister and brother.
    C Yes, I did.

19 What time does the film start?

    A At 7.00, I think.
    B Tom Cruise and Madonna.
    C When did you go?

20 What's the date today?

    A The 15th, I think.
    B It's 2002.
    C It's Tuesday.

CLUES

Question 16: Look at the question word *What*.

Question 17: The question asks *Where* – you need a place.

Question 18: *Who* – look for a person or a name.

Question 19: *When* – look for a time or a date.

Question 20: The question asks for the *date*, not the day – look for an answer with the date of the month in it, for example, 3rd (third), 18th (eighteenth).

Part 3 – everyday conversations

■ For **questions 21 – 25**, you complete a longer conversation.

■ You choose from a list of options. There are five spaces and eight options.

■ The conversation may take place in a shop or restaurant, at school, on the telephone, etc.

■ One speaker may want to complain about something, make arrangements, ask for information, order food, etc.

1 ⟩ Read the instructions to the exam task opposite.

1 Who are the speakers? Where does the conversation take place?
2 Where do you mark your answers in the exam?

2 ⟩ Look at the example 0. Why is E the right answer?

1 What question does the assistant ask?
2 What can we say to answer this question?
3 What is the customer's problem?

3 ⟩ Skills focus: choosing the right option

You should always read the line **after** the gap before you choose your answer.

Read the whole conversation. Then tick the best answer a) or b).

Teacher: Hello, Elena. What are you looking for?
Elena: a) I need some information for a sports project.
            b) I can't find my library ticket.
Teacher: We've got a new video about famous sportspeople. Would you like to watch it?
Elena: a) Are there any books about sport?
            b) Yes, but I have to go to class now. Can I take it home?
Teacher: Of course you can, but you must return it tomorrow.
Elena: Thanks very much. I will.

4 ⟩ Read the gapped conversation opposite. Don't read the options yet.

1 What does the assistant ask the customer about the CD player?
2 What does the assistant offer to do?
3 What does the customer decide to do? How do you know?

5 ⟩ Complete the conversation by choosing from the options.

1 Read each line. What kind of answer fits each gap? Use the clues to help you decide.
2 Read the next line to check your answer.

6 ⟩ Communication: role play

Practise similar conversations.

Student A: You bought a pair of jeans last week. The zip has broken. You would like to change them for another pair.
Student B: You bought a bag yesterday. It cost £12.50. The handle has come off. You would like your money back.

Part 3

Questions 21 – 25

Complete the conversation.
What does the customer say to the shop assistant?
For questions 21 – 25, mark the correct letter A – H on the answer sheet.

EXAMPLE	ANSWER
Assistant: Good afternoon. Can I help you?	
Customer: **0**	**E**

Assistant: Oh dear. And what's the problem exactly?

Customer: **21** ....

Assistant: I see. When did you buy it?

Customer: **22** ....

Assistant: Yes, please. Well, I can give you your money back or change the CD player for a new one.

Customer: **23** ....

Assistant: Certainly. Can you write your name on this form for me, please?

Customer: **24** ....

Assistant: Thank you very much. Here's your money, £89.50.

Customer: **25** ....

Assistant: You're welcome. Goodbye.

A I only bought it last week. Do you want the receipt?

B Three days ago.

C Of course. Here you are.

D Thank you very much for your help.

E Yes, please. I bought this CD player here and there's something wrong with it.

F Do you want me to pay?

G I think I'd like my money back, please.

H Well, when I turn it on, it doesn't always work.

CLUES

Question 21: Which option talks about a *problem*?

Question 22: Be careful! Both **A** and **B** look possible, but look at the next thing the assistant says: 'Yes, please.'

Question 23: The assistant offers two things. What does the customer choose?

Question 24: The assistant asks the customer to do something. What does the customer reply?

Question 25: When somebody gives you something, what do you say?

Part 4 – factual text

■ For **questions 26 – 32**, you read a short text (about 200 words).

■ You answer questions about it. Sometimes you have to choose the right answer **A, B or C.**

■ The text may have some words you don't know, but you can still answer the questions.

1 ⟩ Look at the instructions and the title of the text opposite.

1 How many questions are there?
2 What is the text about?
3 What do you have to do in this task?
4 Where do you mark your answers in the exam?

2 ⟩ Look at the words in the box. Which words do you think are in the text? Tick them.

Add five more words which you think are in the text.

> manager   supermarket   shop
> fruit and vegetables   emails
> money   meetings   assistant

3 ⟩ Look through the text quickly. Check your answers to exercise 2. Were you right?

4 ⟩ Read the text carefully. Answer these questions. <u>Underline</u> the answers in the text.

1 Where was Jonathan's first job?
2 What company does he work for now?
3 What was his first job with the company? What is his job now?
4 What does Jonathan do most of the time in his job?
5 When did Jonathan start and finish work last week?
6 When will he start and finish this week?
7 What does he do before anything else every day?
8 What is his favourite part of the job?
9 What does he do when he gets back from a journey?
10 Does Jonathan like his job?

5 ⟩ Look at the example 0. Why is C the correct answer?

1 Read the first sentence in the text. Which words tell you C is the right answer?
2 Look at **A.** Did Jonathan work while he was at college, according to the text?
3 Look at **B.** Did Jonathan work for his father **before** or **after** he worked for Bargain Foods?

6 ⟩ Read the questions and do the exam task. Use the clues to help you.

CLUES

Question 26: What did Jonathan do when he *joined Saver Mall*?

Question 27: Saver Mall is in London, but is Jonathan there all the time?

Question 28: Last week Jonathan worked from 3 p.m. to 11 p.m., but this week he is working from 7 a.m. to 3 p.m. Which is the best answer?

Question 29: Does the text tell you **when** Jonathan goes to meetings? Does it tell you when he checks other supermarkets?

Question 30: Look for another way of saying *like best*.

Question 31: Find the word *journey* in the text.

Question 32: Look for another way of saying *enjoys his job*. What does the text tell you about *money*? Does it say that Jonathan wants more?

Part 4

Questions 26 – 32

Read the article about a supermarket manager and then answer the questions.
For questions 26 – 32, mark A, B or C on the answer sheet.

The life of a supermarket manager

Jonathan Matthews left school at seventeen, went to college and then worked in his father's mini-market. After two years, he went to work for Bargain Foods and then he joined Saver Mall as a trainee manager. Three years later he got his present job as a supermarket manager with Saver Mall.

This is what he told us about his job:

'The supermarket where I am manager is in west London but I spend most of my time travelling by road to Saver Mall supermarkets all over Britain. I need to see things in our other supermarkets. I also go to lots of meetings.

My work hours change every week because Saver Mall is open 24 hours a day. Last week I worked from 3 p.m. to 11 p.m. but this week I need to be at work from 7 a.m. to 3 p.m. The first thing I do each day is check my emails.

Sometimes I go to different countries to check how supermarkets are doing. That's my favourite part of the job! But I like my work in London too. Travelling can be very hard work. When I get back from a journey, I usually go straight to bed. I earn quite good money and I'm happy working for Saver Mall.'

SUPERMARKET

EXAMPLE			ANSWER
0 Jonathan's first job was			
A at college. **B** with Bargain Foods. **C** in a mini-market.			**C**

26 When Jonathan first worked for Saver Mall, he was

    A an assistant.   **B** a manager.   **C** a trainee manager.

27 Jonathan does most of his work

    A in London.   **B** in other countries.   **C** in other supermarkets.

28 Jonathan's working hours

    A are different each week.   **B** are 3 p.m. to 11 p.m.   **C** are 7 a.m. to 3 p.m.

29 At the beginning of each day, Jonathan

    A goes to a meeting.   **B** checks other supermarkets.   **C** reads messages.

30 What does Jonathan like best?

    A checking emails   **B** going to different countries   **C** travelling by road

31 The first thing Jonathan does after a journey is

    A have a meal.   **B** go to his office.   **C** go to bed.

32 Jonathan

    A enjoys his job.   **B** does not like his work in London.   **C** wants to earn more money.

Part 5 – gapped text

- For **questions 33 – 40**, you read a short factual text with eight numbered spaces.
- You choose **one** word **A**, **B** or **C** to fill each space.
- This part tests your grammar.

1 〉 Read the instructions and the title of the text opposite.

1 What is the text about?
2 How many questions are there?
3 Where do you mark your answers in the exam?

2 〉 Look at the example 0. Why is C the correct answer?

1 Look at **A**. Can we say *going on train*? What word is missing?
2 Look at **B**. Is *going to train* possible? Is *train* a verb?

3 〉 Grammar focus: prepositions

a 〉 Fill in the spaces with the correct preposition: at/by/from/in/on/to.

1 Do you live .... a town or a village?
2 Which month were you born .... ?
3 Do you go to school .... bus or .... foot?
4 How far is it .... your house .... school?
5 What time does your father get home .... night?
6 If you have a problem, who do you talk .... ?

b 〉 Ask and answer the questions with a partner.

4 〉 Grammar focus: quantity words

For this part, you need to know what kind of words we can use before countable and uncountable nouns.

a 〉 Complete the table with words from the list.

some/any/much/many/few/little/lots of/no

Countable			Uncountable		
some	....	passengers	*some*	....	food
....	....	windows	....	....	time
....	....		....	....	

b 〉 Underline the correct word in each pair.

Hawaii, which is in the middle of the Pacific Ocean, is the USA's fiftieth state. In fact, Hawaii is made up of **(1)** *a few/lots of* islands (about two thousand!), with beautiful beaches, clean water, tropical forests, and even **(2)** *some/any* volcanoes! There is plenty to do and see in Hawaii. **(3)** *Much/Many* people go to see the famous humpback whales between the months of November and April, and **(4)** *many/few* surfers can stay away from the beaches for very long! There isn't **(5)** *any/some* chance of going hungry in Hawaii: Hawaiian people love to eat well and their diet includes **(6)** *much/lots of* fish and meat, as well as different types of vegetables and fruit.

5 〉 Read the whole text opposite. Ignore the spaces.

Why do people enjoy travelling by train?

6 〉 Now do the task. Use the clues to help you.

7 〉 Read the text again. Do your answers make sense?

Part 5

Questions 33 – 40

Read the article about trains.
Choose the best word (A, B or C) for each space (33 – 40).
For questions 33 – 40, mark A, B or C on the answer sheet.

TRAINS – THE BEST WAY TO TRAVEL

For many people, going ____**0**____ train is the most exciting way
to travel. You don't have to wait ____**33**____ hours at the airport
with thousands ____**34**____ other passengers. You just go ____**35**____
the railway station a few minutes before the train ____**36**____ ,
buy a ticket, get on the train, and the journey begins!

You can look at things ____**37**____ the windows, have a sleep, read a book
or go for a walk up and down the train. There is usually someone interesting
to talk ____**38**____ and when you get hungry, you can eat your picnic! If you
didn't bring ____**39**____ picnic with you, there's often a restaurant or small
café on the train where you can buy ____**40**____ food and a drink.

EXAMPLE						ANSWER
0	**A** on		**B** to		**C** by	**C**

33	**A**	for	**B**	in	**C**	at
34	**A**	and	**B**	from	**C**	of
35	**A**	at	**B**	to	**C**	in
36	**A**	will leave	**B**	left	**C**	leaves
37	**A**	by	**B**	through	**C**	inside
38	**A**	for	**B**	at	**C**	to
39	**A**	a	**B**	some	**C**	the
40	**A**	a	**B**	any	**C**	some

CLUES

Question 33: Which preposition do you use with a period of time like hours, months, years?

Question 34: Which preposition do we use after *thousands*?

Question 35: You need a preposition of direction, not place.

Question 36: Which verb tense follows words like *when*, *after*, *before* – present or future?

Question 37: Where are the things you look at?

Question 38: You need a preposition after *talk* – which one?

Question 39: Is *picnic* countable or uncountable? Do you need a definite or indefinite article?

Question 40: Is *food* countable or uncountable? Is the sentence negative or positive?

- For **questions 41–50**, you read a short text with ten numbered spaces. The text is a short letter or note.
- You have to think of **one** word for each space.
- You must spell the words correctly.
- This part tests your grammar and vocabulary.

1 〉 *Vocabulary focus:* what kind of word?

You have to write a content word in some spaces. You should read the whole sentence carefully to make sure you understand the meaning, and decide what kind of word you need.

a 〉 *Read the sentences. What kind of word do you need in each space?* <u>Underline</u> *the correct option in brackets.*

1   I'm learning English in Brighton and I can ………. (*noun*/<u>*verb*</u>) it much better now.

2   I have a nice big ………. (*adjective*/*noun*) with a bed and a desk.

3   The food is a little ………. (*verb*/*adjective*), but it's not too bad.

4   I have to ………. (*verb*/*adverb*) up at eight o'clock each morning.

5   My ………. (*verb*/*noun*) is called Rob and he's from Scotland.

b 〉 *Now complete the sentences with the words in the box.*

teacher   room   speak   strange   get

2 〉 *Grammar focus:* verb forms

Sometimes you have to write a verb in the space in the present or past tense. Sometimes you write part of a verb. You should look for clues that tell you what tense you need.

a 〉 *Circle the correct verb form. Use the <u>underlined</u> words to help you decide which verb form is correct.*

1   I *walk*/*am walking* to school <u>every day</u>.

2   My brother *plays*/*is playing* football <u>at the moment</u>.

3   <u>Yesterday</u> I *went*/*was going* to the park in the afternoon.

4   We *were doing*/*did* our homework <u>when Peter arrived</u>.

5   I *arrived*/*have arrived* in London <u>two weeks ago.</u>

6   I *have been*/*am* in London <u>for two weeks</u>.

7   I *didn't buy*/*haven't bought* any presents for my family <u>yet</u>.

8   Let's meet tomorrow because I *will go*/*am going* back to my country <u>on Friday</u>.

9   I forgot to return your CD. I *will bring*/*am bringing* it to your house <u>next weekend</u>.

10   <u>Tonight</u> I *will go*/*am going* to the cinema with some friends.

b 〉 *Complete the sentences with a verb or part of a verb.*

1   What time are you ………. to visit me tomorrow?

2   There ………. only one more day until my holiday!

3   I ………. write to you again very soon.

4   We ………. a lot of sightseeing in London last week.

5   At the moment, I ………. reading a book about South America.

3 Grammar focus: personal pronouns

This part may test personal pronouns, e.g. *I/me/my/mine*, *you/your/yours*, etc.

Write a pronoun in each space. Choose A, B or C.

1	Those shoes are	A my	B mine	C me
2	Darren and Lucy invited us to .... house for dinner.	A their	B they	C theirs
3	.... new chairs are the same as those ones over there.	A We	B Ours	C Our
4	Are these books .... or Rod's?	A you	B your	C yours
5	Has Francesca opened .... birthday presents yet?	A she	B hers	C her

4 Grammar focus: articles and pronouns

We use *a* the first time we talk about something, and *the* for the second time.

Example: I went to **a** good party. I will tell you about **the** party tomorrow.

With some words, we always use *the*.

Example: The sun is very hot. (there is only one sun)

We use pronouns so we don't have to repeat words.

Example: John saw the film yesterday and **he** liked **it** a lot.

Complete the text opposite. Write an article or pronoun in each space.

Dear Marina,

I'm having (1) .... fantastic time here in France. I'm staying in (2) .... small town by (3) .... seaside with my pen friend's family. Yesterday, my friend and (4) .... went to (5) .... beach and tomorrow (6) .... are going shopping for presents.

On Saturday, we bought (7) .... sightseeing ticket and went round (8) .... town on (9) .... bus – (10) .... was great fun!

I will be home next Saturday. See you soon.

Bye for now.

Julia

5 Grammar focus: conjunctions

You need to know how to join ideas together, e.g.:
and We went to the zoo **and** saw lots of animals.
or We can go to the cinema **or** to the disco.
but I wanted to go swimming **but** it was too cold.
because I didn't go out **because** I was sick.
so She was tired **so** she went to bed.

Complete the sentences with the right conjunction.

1 I wanted to come to the party .... I wasn't feeling very well.
2 We're going to the cinema .... then we're going to the disco.
3 We didn't go to the park .... it started to rain.
4 The traffic was very bad .... we decided to walk.
5 You can catch a bus .... you can take a train – they take the same time.

6 Spelling focus

Read the note and the student's answers. Correct the spelling mistakes.

Dear Marios,

Thanks __41__ letting me stay in __42__ house last weekend. I had a __43__ time. __44__ is so much to do in Edinburgh! When are you __45__ to Oxford? I've found a new burger bar __46__ plays fantastic music – you'll love it!

Tomorrow I want to play football but I have __47__ much homework. I hope I can finish everything __48__ lunchtime.

Write to me soon and let me __49__ when you are free to visit. Good luck __50__ your exams!

41	four
42	you're
43	grate
44	Their
45	comming
46	wich
47	to
48	befor
49	no
50	wiht

7 ⟩ *Read the instructions to the exam task below.*

1 What kind of text is it: a letter, a newspaper article, a note?
2 How many questions are there?
3 Where do you mark your answers in the exam?

8 ⟩ *Read the text quickly.*

1 Who is the letter from?
2 Who is the letter to?
3 What is the letter about?

9 ⟩ *Do the exam task. Read each sentence and decide what kind of word goes in each space. Use the clues to help you.*

EXAM PRACTICE

Part 6

Questions 41 – 50

Complete the letter.
Write ONE word in each space (41 – 50).
For questions 41 – 50, write your words on the answer sheet.

Dear Christina,

How are (**Example:** ___you___)? I am sorry you could __41__ come on the school trip yesterday. Peter told __42__ that you were feeling ill and you __43__ to stay at home. I hope you __44__ feeling better now.

We all thought __45__ was a great day out: more fun than going to __46__ and doing lessons! I got home __47__ nine o'clock and went to bed immediately __48__ I was so tired.

Are you __49__ to school on Monday? I __50__ tell you everything about the trip when I see you.

Lots of love,

Melina

CLUES

Question 41: Could Christina come on the school trip?

Question 42: What pronoun do we use after the verb *tell*?

Question 43: Which modal verb do you need? Did Christina **want** to stay in bed all day?

Question 44: Look at the verb *feeling*. What tense is this?

Question 45: You need a pronoun here.

Question 46: Where do you *do lessons*?

Question 47: You need a preposition. Which one?

Question 48: What word can join the two parts of the sentence together?

Question 49: Which verb can you use here?

Question 50: What do you use to make the future tense?

Part 7 – completing a form

■ For **questions 51 – 55**, you read a short text (about 50 words).

■ Then you complete a form using information from the text.

■ You do not need to write sentences – only words and short phrases.

■ Correct spelling and use of capital letters are essential.

For this part you often need to know: surname, date of birth, age, nationality, address, foreign languages, occupation, etc.

You also have to spell words correctly and use capital letters correctly.

1 〉 *Vocabulary focus:* **nationalities**

Complete the table. Don't forget to use capital letters!

Country	Nationality	Language
France	French..........	....
Germany	....	....
Italy	....	Italian..........
Mexico	....	....
Russia	....	....
Spain	....	....
USA	....	....
Argentina	....	....
Japan	....	....

2 〉 *Vocabulary focus:* **dates**

a 〉 *Look at the examples. Say the dates 1 – 4 to a partner.*

Examples: 25th January 1986   The twenty-fifth of January, nineteen eighty-six
        8th August 2002   The eighth of August, two thousand and two

1   13th July 1991   ....
2   30th September 1985   ....
3   1st April 1977   ....
4   18th December 2010   ....

b 〉 *We can write dates in different ways. Look at the example. Then write the dates 1 – 4 above in two other ways. Don't forget to use capital letters!*

Example: 25th January 1986   25 January 1986   25/1/86

c 〉 *Ask and answer the questions.*

1   When were you born?   2   When were your sisters and brothers born?

3 〉 *Vocabulary focus:* **occupations**

Write the occupations in Column B. Do we write jobs with a capital letter?

A	B
This person ...	**so he's/she's a ...**
manages	...manager....
teaches	....
studies	....
works on a farm	....
writes books	....
works in a bank	....

4 > Read the instructions to the exam task below.

1 Who are you going to read about?
2 What do they want?
3 What do you have to do?
4 How many questions are there?
5 Where do you have to write the information in the exam?

5 > Look at the form which a student completed. Find and correct the mistakes. Use the clues to help you.

Read the information about Mr and Mrs Arnold. They want a student who is learning English to stay in their house.
Fill in the information on the application form.
For questions 51 – 55, write the information on the answer sheet.

Malcolm Arnold lives at 27, River Road, Cambridge. He writes books. His wife teaches English. Mr Arnold was born on 20th March 1971, and Mrs Arnold on 8th November 1972. They would like two students from Spain to stay with them.

Application Form for a student guest

Surname:	51	malcolm arnold
Address:	52	Rever Road 27, Cambrige
Occupation: wife:	53	She teaches english
husband:		writer
Date of birth: wife:		8/11/72
husband:	54	3/20/1971
Nationality of students:	55	from Spain

CLUES

Question 51: The student wrote both names and he forgot to use capital letters.

Question 52: Look back at the information about Malcolm Arnold. Is the address spelled correctly?

Question 53: Mrs Arnold teaches English so what's her *occupation*? *She's an* … . Did the student use a capital letter?

Question 54: Check the date carefully. Look at the order of the numbers.

Question 55: If you come from Spain, what's your *nationality*?

6 > *Read the instructions to the exam task below.*

1   Who are you going to read about?
2   What kind of form do you have to fill in?

7 > *Do the exam task. Use the clues to help you.*

Part 7

Questions 51 – 55

Read the information about David.
Fill in the information on the Job Application Form for him.
For questions 51 – 55, write the information on the answer sheet.

David Cassidy is sixteen years old. He's from the USA. He wants to work from 1st July to 31st August. He worked in a language school during his holidays last year. He has lived in France and speaks the language well.

Job Application Form

First name:	David
Surname:	51
Age:	52
Nationality:	53
Dates:	54 1/7 –
Foreign languages:	55
Have you worked in a language school before?	Yes.

CLUES

Question 51: Remember to use capital letters and check your spelling.

Question 52: You can use letters or numbers. Check your spelling!

Question 53: Check your answer in Exercise 1 on page 23.

Question 54: Use numbers here.

Question 55: The information does not say *foreign languages* so what do you need to look for?

Part 8 – continuous writing

■ This part tests your writing skills.

■ You may have to write a notice or a short message to someone.

■ There are 3 – 4 different things to write about.

1 > *Read the instructions for the writing task below.*

1 What do you have to write in this task?
2 How many questions do you have to answer? What are the questions?
3 How many words should you write?
4 Where do you write your answers in the exam?

You have lost your Discman. Write a notice to put on the wall of your school.

Say:

– **where** you lost your Discman

– **what** your Discman **looks like** and **how** to return
  it to you

Write 20 – 25 words.
Write your notice on the back of the answer sheet.

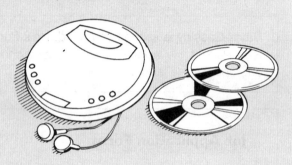

2 > *Read the example answers below. Ignore the <u>underlined</u> mistakes for now.*

1 Which example does not answer all the questions?   .....
2 Which one answers all the questions but is too long?   .....
3 Which one is about the right length and answers all the questions?   .....

A

I <u>am lose</u> my
Discman. I want it
back. <u>Its</u> cost £195.
If <u>you</u> <u>found</u> it,
please tell me.

Thanks.

Fran

B

LOST in <u>clasroom</u> 3D
on <u>saturday</u>!
A blue and <u>wite</u>
Discman with a CD
inside.
If you find it, please
return it⟨me in the
<u>brake</u> on <u>Wenesday</u>.

<u>Tank</u> you.

Marios.

C

I <u>losed</u> my new Discman
in the <u>ofice</u> two days
<u>before</u>. It is new and
white. <u>Their</u> is a Bon
Jovi CD in it I think.
If you <u>are finding</u> it,
please give it back to
me. I will be <u>on</u> classroom
5A <u>the</u> next Thursday
at 4 o'clock. Please
bring it.

Thank you very much.

Marina.

3 ⟩ Correct the mistakes in the sample answers.

A	B		C	
1	1	5	1	5 ....
2	2	6	2	6 ....
3	3	7	3	7 ....
	4		4	

4 ⟩ Read the exam task below.

1 What do you have to write in this task?
2 How many things do you have to write about? <u>Underline</u> them.
3 How will you start your note? Which choice below is not correct? Cross it out.

Hi, (NAME)!
Dear (NAME),
My friend (NAME),
(NAME),

---

5 ⟩ Write your note.

6 ⟩ Check your writing carefully.

- Have you answered all the questions?
- Have you written about 20 – 25 (maximum 30) words?
- Have you signed your note?
- Is your spelling correct?
- Have you used capital letters for names, etc.?

EXAM PRACTICE

Part 8
Question 56

Yesterday you left your friend's book on the bus when you went home.

Write a note to your friend.

Tell him/her:

– what you lost

– when and **where** you lost it

– that you want to replace it

Write 20 – 25 words.
Write your note on the back of the answer sheet.

PAPER 2   Listening   (approximately 25 minutes)

PREPARATION

Part 1 – five short dialogues

- For **questions 1 – 5**, you hear five short conversations.
- The conversations are between friends or relatives, or take place in a shop, at a ticket office, etc.
- You listen and choose the correct picture **A**, **B** or **C**.

In this part there may be questions about numbers, prices, times, shapes and sizes.

1 ▷ 🔲 *Pronunciation focus:* **numbers**

Listen to the recording. Tick (✔) the number you hear.

1 a) 13 ✔   b) 30
2 a) 19   b) 90
3 a) 50   b) 15
4 a) 17   b) 70
5 a) 40   b) 14
6 a) 18   b) 80
7 a) 25   b) 55

2 ▷ *Vocabulary focus:* **prices**

a ▷ *Match the words and the prices. Write the numbers next to the words.*

| £16.95   £50.25   30p   £60.13   £5.25 |

1 five pounds, twenty-five pence   £5.25
2 sixteen pounds, ninety-five pence   ....
3 thirty pence   ....
4 sixty pounds, thirteen pence   ....
5 fifty pounds, twenty-five pence   ....

b ▷ 🔲 *How much do they cost? Listen and write the prices. Write figures, not words.*

c ▷ *Ask and answer the questions.*

1   How much do the things in exercise 2b▷ cost in your country?
2   Which things are cheaper in your country? Which are more expensive?

3 〉 Vocabulary focus: *ways of telling the time*

There are different ways of telling the time.

Examples: | `12.30` | twelve thirty

| `8.40` | twenty to nine   OR   eight forty

a〉 *Match the times to the clocks.*

two o'clock   quarter to eight   ten past six   half past three

| `3.30` | | `6.10` | | `7.45` | | `2.00` |

1 .... 　 2 .... 　 3 .... 　 4 ....

b〉 *Ask and answer. Say the times 1–3 in a different way.*

A: What's the time?
B: It's ...

c〉 *Listen and tick the correct clock.*

1　a) | `9.15` |　　b) | `9.50` |

2　a) | `10.25` |　　b) | `9.35` |

3　a) | `3.30` |　　b) | `2.30` |

4　a) | `11.45` |　　b) | `12.15` |

5　a) | `8.35` |　　b) | `8.25` |

4 〉 Vocabulary focus: **shapes**

a〉 *Label the shapes. Use the words in the box.*

triangle   rectangle   square   circle

1 .... 　 2 .... 　 3 .... 　 4 ....

b〉 *Answer the questions. Use the adjectives in the box.*

square   round/circular   rectangular

What shape is ...

1　a football?　　...................
2　a tennis court?　　...................
3　your classroom?　　...................
4　your bedroom?　　...................

5 🔊 *Read and listen to the instructions to the exam task below.*

1 How many conversations are there?
2 How many pictures are there for each conversation?
3 How many times will you hear each conversation?
4 How do you mark your answers?

6 🔊 *Look at the example and listen to the recording.*

1 What is the question?
2 What is the answer?
3 How do you know?

7 🔊 *Listen to the rest of the recording and answer questions 1 – 5.*

EXAM PRACTICE

Part 1

Questions 1 – 5

Listen to the tape.
You will hear five short conversations.
You will hear each conversation twice.
There is one question for each conversation.
For questions 1 – 5, put a tick ✔ under the right answer.

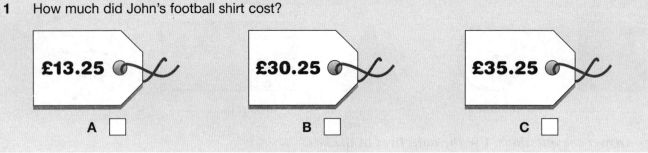

EXAMPLE

0 What time is it?

04.00	05.00	08.00
A ☐	B ✔	C ☐

1 How much did John's football shirt cost?

£13.25	£30.25	£35.25
A ☐	B ☐	C ☐

2 Which cake does the woman want?

A ☐   B ☐   C ☐

3 What size shoe does the man take?

SIZE: 2

SIZE: 8

SIZE: 9

A ☐   B ☐   C ☐

4 When is Anna's birthday?

13th September

30th September

13th November

A ☐   B ☐   C ☐

5 What is Petros going to buy?

A ☐   B ☐   C ☐

Part 2 – conversation

■ For **questions 6 – 10**, you hear a conversation between two people. The two people sometimes know each other.

■ You have to match two lists, for example, names of people with activities they like doing.

1〉 *Read the instructions to the exam task opposite.*

1   How many questions are there?
2   Who is talking?
3   What is the conversation about?
4   What do you have to match?
5   How many activities are there for matching?
6   How many times will you hear the conversation?
7   Look at the example. How do you mark your answers?

2〉 *Vocabulary focus:* **free time activities**

a〉 *Look at the pictures. What are they doing?*

Example: 'In picture 1, they are visiting a museum.'

b〉 *What do you like doing best in your free time? Tick (✔) three pictures.*

c〉 *Ask and answer questions.*

Example:

1   A: How often do you go to museums?
     B: Never!

| Every day/weekend | Once/Twice a week/month | Quite often | Sometimes | Never |

3〉 *Vocabulary focus:* **the weather**

In the exam, you may hear people talking about the weather.

a〉 🔲 *Listen to the conversation. Match the days and the weather.*

1   Saturday morning   a) It was hot and sunny.
2   Saturday afternoon   b) It was cold and windy.
3   Sunday morning   c) It rained.

b〉 *Ask and answer questions.*

What was the weather like in your town yesterday? on Monday? last Saturday?

4〉 [cassette icon] *Do the exam task. Answer questions 6 – 10.*

5〉 *Compare your answers with other students. Are they the same?*

6〉 [cassette icon] *Listen again. Check your answers. Add any that you missed the first time.*

EXAM PRACTICE

Part 2
Questions 6 – 10

Listen to Paul talking to Jane about his holiday in Scotland.
What did he do on each day?

For questions 6 – 10, write a letter A – H next to each day.
You will hear the conversation twice.

EXAMPLE

0   Saturday $\boxed{\text{E}}$

DAYS

6   Sunday   ☐

7   Monday   ☐

8   Tuesday   ☐

9   Wednesday   ☐

10   Thursday   ☐

ACTIVITIES

A   bicycle ride

B   football

C   museum

D   visit to another city

E   shopping

F   studying for exams

G   swimming

H   playing computer games

Part 3 – conversation

- For **questions 11–15**, you hear a conversation between two people.
- Sometimes the people know each other. Sometimes the conversation takes place in a shop, at a travel agent's, etc.
- You have to answer five questions by choosing **A**, **B** or **C**.

1 〉 Read the instructions to the exam task opposite.

1 Who is talking?
3 How do you mark your answers?
2 What is the conversation about?
4 How many times do you hear the conversation?

In the exam, you may need to understand simple descriptions of objects. You may hear people talking about dimensions, size and shape.

2 〉 Vocabulary focus: measurements

a〉 Listen to the recording. Look at the measurements in the box. Tick (✔) the ones you hear.

| 15m | 2m 80cm | 50cm | 1m 30cm | 1m 90cm | 5m 95cm | 9m 20cm | 8m |

b〉 Write these measurements in figures.

1 three metres seventy-five ....
4 two metres five ....

2 eighty centimetres ....
5 three metres thirty ....

3 one metre twenty-five ....

3 〉 Vocabulary focus: describing things

a〉 Put the words in the box into the right groups.

| wood jacket long wardrobe wide wool |
| short high scarf tall belt plastic deep |
| nylon pencil case leather watch cotton |

A	B	C
Size	Material	Objects

b〉 Circle the correct word in each question.

1 How *long/deep* is that table? ......1m 75cm......

2 How *tall/high* is Nick? ....

3 Will the wardrobe go through the door? How *tall/high* is it? ....

4 How *deep/long* is that skirt? ....

5 How *high/deep* is a tennis net at each end? ....

c〉 Listen to the recording and write the answers to the questions in figures.

d〉 Look at the objects in Box C. Which ones do you have? What are they made of?

Example: My watch is plastic.

4 〉 Do the exam task. Listen to the recording and answer questions 11–15.

5 〉 Compare your answers with other students. Are they the same?

6 〉 Listen again. Check your answers. Add any that you missed the first time.

Part 3

Questions 11–15

Listen to John phoning a shop about something he wants to buy.

For questions 11–15, tick ✔ A, B or C.
You will hear the conversation twice.

EXAMPLE

0   The shop is in

A	Chester Avenue.	☐
B	Market Road.	☐
C	Oxford Street.	✔

---

11   John wants to buy

A	a tent.	☐
B	a rucksack.	☐
C	a bag.	☐

12   The Weekender Plus is

A	40cm by 60cm.	☐
B	70cm by 90cm.	☐
C	60cm by 90cm.	☐

13   The shop only sells rucksacks made of

A	nylon.	☐
B	plastic.	☐
C	canvas.	☐

14   John is going to buy a

A	red and green rucksack.	☐
B	blue and white rucksack.	☐
C	green and blue rucksack.	☐

15   The rucksack costs

A	£29.95.	☐
B	£39.95.	☐
C	£13.95.	☐

Part 4 – conversation

- For **questions 16 – 20**, you hear a conversation.
- Conversations often take place in shops, offices, etc.
- You listen and write down missing information in a message or notes.
- You write one or two words or numbers.
- Spelling is not tested but you should spell simple words correctly.

1 ⟩ Read the instructions to the exam task opposite.

1 How many questions are there?
2 Who are you going to hear?
3 What is the speaker going to talk about?
4 Where do you write your answers?
5 How many times will you hear the conversation?

2 ⟩ Read the notes. What kind of information is missing? Match the questions with a) – e).

Question 16   a) a name
Question 17   b) something to eat
Question 18   c) a time
Question 19   d) a price
Question 20   e) a place

3 ⟩ 🎞️ Listen to the recording and try to complete as many answers as possible.

4 ⟩ 🎞️ Listen again. Check your answers. Add any that you missed the first time.

5 ⟩ Check your answers.

1 How many words did you write in each space?   2 Is the spelling correct?

6 ⟩ Communication: ordering food and drink

a ⟩ Complete the dialogue with words and phrases from the box.

I'd like   for   Can I have   some   anything   a

Waiter: Would you like a starter?

Customer: Yes, please. I'll have .... salad Nicoise.

Waiter: And for the main course?

Customer: .... the vegetable soup, please?

Waiter: Certainly. Would you like something .... dessert?

Customer: Hmm, ... cheese, I think.

Waiter: And would you like .... to drink?

Customer: Yes, ... a coke, please.

Waiter: Thank you.

b ⟩ 🎞️ Listen and check your answers.

c ⟩ In pairs or groups, order a meal from the menu.

BLUE SKY RESTAURANT
3-course lunch only £8.95

Starters
Salad Nicoise (lettuce, tuna, olives, egg)
Fresh fruit surprise

Main course
Vegetable soup
Fish and chips with peas
Hamburger and side salad
Blue Sky pizza

Dessert
Ice cream
Chocolate cake
Selection of cheeses

Drinks
Coke
Mineral water
Coffee or tea

Part 4

Questions 16 – 20

You will hear a tourist guide talking to some tourists about places to have lunch in Bournemouth.

Listen and complete questions 16 – 20.
You will hear the conversation twice.

LUNCH in BOURNEMOUTH

Tourists free until:	**16**	_o'clock_
Fast food restaurants:	**17**	_near the_
Seafood meal costs:	**18**	£
Name of hotel:	**19**	
Hotel lunch costs:		_£8.95_
If you don't want to sit down, buy:	**20**	_and chips_

Part 5 – factual monologue

- For **questions 21 – 25**, you hear a monologue.
- The monologue is often a recorded telephone message.
- You listen and fill in missing information in a message or notes.
- You write one or two words or numbers.
- Spelling is not tested but you should spell simple words correctly.

1 ⟩ Read the instructions to the exam task opposite.

1 How many questions are there?
2 What are you going to hear?
3 Where do you write your answers?
4 How many times will you hear the information?

2 ⟩ Read the notes. What kind of information is missing? Match the questions with a) – e).

Question 21   a) something to eat
Question 22   b) a telephone number
Question 23   c) a time
Question 24   d) a price
Question 25   e) a kind of visitor

3 ⟩ Vocabulary focus: telephone numbers

In the exam, you often need to understand and write down telephone numbers.

a ⟩ 🔊 Read the conversations. Then listen and write the telephone numbers.

1 A: What's Maria's new phone number?
   B: Sorry, I don't know.
   C: It's ....

2 A: Can you remember Christos' mobile number?
   B: Yes, it's ....
   A: OK, I'll give him a ring now.

3 A: John, have you got the number for the Mega Screen Cinema?
   B: Wait a minute. Let me look in the phone book. Here it is. ....
   A: Thanks.

4 A: Hello, is that .... ?
   B: No, this is 01223 88 55 22.
   A: Sorry, wrong number.

5 A: Hello, Directory Enquiries, which town please?
   B: Can you tell me the number of the Football News Service, please?
   A: The number you require is ....

b ⟩ Check your answers with a partner.

c ⟩ Ask and answer. Write the numbers.

What's   1 your phone number?   ....
         2 your mother's/father's phone number at work?   ....
         3 the phone number of your school?   ....
         4 the phone number of the local sports centre?   ....

4 ❯ 📼 *Listen to the recording and do the exam task. Try to complete as many answers as possible.*

5 ❯ 📼 *Listen again. Check your answers. Add any you missed the first time.*

6 ❯ *Check your answers.*

1   How many words did you write in each space?
2   Is the spelling correct?

EXAM PRACTICE

Part 5

Questions 21 – 25

You will hear some information about a museum.

Listen and complete questions 21 – 25.
You will hear the information twice.

The WINCHESTER MUSEUM

Museum is open:	Monday to Saturday
From:	9 a.m.
To:	**21** _____ p.m.
Students pay:	£4.40
Children pay:	**22** £ _____
Special prices for:	**23** groups and _____
Café serves:	**24** _____ and snacks
For more information, call:	**25** Winchester _____

PAPER 3   Speaking   (8 – 10 minutes)

PREPARATION

Part 1 – personal, factual information

- This part is 5 – 6 minutes.
- You will probably be with one other student.
- One examiner asks you some questions. The other listens.
- You should be able to:
  - talk about where you come from and what you do (job or studies).
  - answer general personal questions, e.g. about family and friends.
  - answer questions about your daily life, interests and likes.

1 ⟩ *Language focus:* spelling

In Part 1, it is important to know the alphabet in English. You may have to spell your name or address.

a ⟩ **What are the names of these letters?**

A   C   E   G   H   I   J   K   N   Q   U   V   W   X   Y   Z

b ⟩ **What do you say when a letter is repeated, like the e in weekend?**

c ⟩ 📼 **Read and listen to the conversation and <u>underline</u> the correct spelling of the names.**

A: Hello, I'm Susan Summers. What's your name, please?

B: Jason *Quigley/Quickly*.

A: Could you spell your surname for me, please, Jason?

B: Yes, it's *Q-U-I-C-K-L-Y / Q-U-I-G-L-E-Y*.

A: Thank you. And what town do you come from?

B: I live in *Farrington, F-A- double R-I-N-G-T-O-N / Farringdon, F-A- double R-I-N-G-D-O-N*.

A: And what's your address?

B: It's 25, *Latimer/Ladima* Street.

A: How do you spell that, please?

B: *L-A-T-I-M-E-R / L-A-D-I-M-A* Street.

A: Thank you.

d ⟩ **Take turns to practise similar conversations with a partner. Write down your partner's name and address. Then show your partner. Is your spelling correct?**

2 ⟩ *Giving personal information*

a ⟩ *Match the questions and the answers.*

1 **A:** What's the name of your school?
2 **A:** Do you like going to school?

3 **A:** What is your favourite subject at school?
4 **A:** Do you have any brothers and sisters?
5 **A:** What sort of music do you like?
6 **A:** What do you usually do at weekends?

a) **B:** Yes, I have one brother and one sister.
b) **B:** I usually visit my friends and sometimes I go to the cinema.
c) **B:** Yes, I do. I have lots of friends there.
d) **B:** Woodgrange Secondary School. It's near my home.
e) **B:** Geography. It's very interesting.
f) **B:** I like all pop music.

b ⟩ 📼 *Listen and check your answers.*

c ⟩ *Ask and answer the questions in 2a* ⟩*.*

Part 1

> 🔊 **Work with a partner. Listen to the tape. You will hear an examiner asking some questions.**
> **Student A: Listen carefully and answer your questions. Tell your partner the answers.**
> **Student B: Listen carefully and answer your questions. Tell your partner the answers.**

PREPARATION

Part 2 – prompt card activity

- This part lasts 3 – 4 minutes.
- You have to make five questions and ask your partner.
- Then you have to answer your partner's questions.
- The examiners will just listen to you.
- The questions may be about personal information.

1 ⟩ Look at the example exam task and the prompt card below.

a ⟩ Answer the questions.

1 What does A have to do?   3 What does B have to do?
2 What help does A have?   4 Do you have to write anything?

> **A**, ask **B** some questions about **food and drink**. Use the words and pictures on the card to help you. Ask **B** five questions.
> **B**, answer A's questions.

FOOD AND DRINK

Ask your partner questions about food and drink.

breakfast?

usually / drink?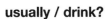

favourite food?

where / dinner?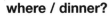

how often?

---

b⟩ **Make questions using these words to help you.**

1 what / you / have / for breakfast?
   What do you have for breakfast?

2 what / you / usually / drink / tea / coffee?

3 what / your / favourite food?

4 where / your family / eat / dinner?

5 how often / you / go to / a restaurant?

c⟩ 🔲 **Listen and check your questions.**

d⟩ **Take turns to ask and answer the questions with a partner. Use the pictures to help you answer.**

2⟩ **Look at another example task below.**

a⟩ **What do you have to ask and answer questions about?**

> **A**, ask **B** some questions about **what he/she does at the weekends.** Use the words and pictures on the card to help you. Ask **B** five questions.
> **B**, answer A's questions.

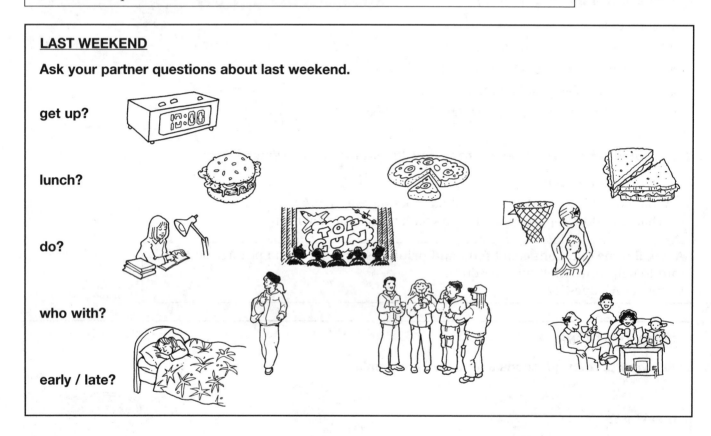

LAST WEEKEND

Ask your partner questions about last weekend.

get up?

lunch?

do?

who with?

early / late?

b⟩ **Correct the grammar mistakes in these questions.**

1 What time did you got up last Saturday?   ....

2 What you ate for lunch?   ....

3 You did your homework?   ....

4 Did you went out with your friends?   ....

5 Went you to bed early or late?   ....

c⟩ 🔲 **Listen and check your answers.**

d⟩ **Take turns to ask and answer the questions with a partner. Use the pictures to help you answer.**

3⟩ **Now do the exam tasks opposite.**

Part 2

Candidate A

A, ask B some questions about **his/her best friend**. Use the words and pictures on the card to help you. Ask B five questions. B, answer A's questions.

BEST FRIEND

Ask your partner about his/her best friend.

name?

live?

favourite food?

hobbies?

why / best friend?

Candidate B

B, ask A some questions about **his/her last holiday**. Use the words and pictures on the card to help you. Ask A five questions. A, answer B's questions.

HOLIDAY ACTIVITIES

Ask your partner about his/her holiday.

where / go?

who / with?

what / do?

weather?

how travel?

TEST 2

PAPER 1   Reading and Writing   (1 hour 10 minutes)

PREPARATION

Part 1 – signs

- For **questions 1–5**, you read signs and notices which you might see in Britain.
- The questions ask:
  Where can you see these notices?   OR   Who are these notices for?
- You choose the correct answer **A**, **B** or **C**.

1〉 *Read the instructions to the exam task opposite.*

1   What question do you have to answer?
2   Where do you mark your answers in the exam?

2〉 *Look at the example 0. Why is B the right answer?*

Do people eat meals in a bank? In a museum?

3〉 *Vocabulary focus:* **people and jobs**

a〉 *Find 11 people or jobs in the word square.*

b〉 *Label the pictures with words from the box.*

P	H	O	T	O	G	R	A	P	H	E	R
A	M	N	O	B	V	C	X	I	Z	A	S
S	D	F	U	G	H	M	J	L	K	L	P
S	O	D	R	I	V	E	R	O	I	U	Y
E	T	R	I	E	W	C	Q	T	A	Z	G
N	V	C	S	D	E	H	E	W	S	X	U
G	F	R	T	T	F	A	N	K	R	M	E
E	I	C	L	E	A	N	E	R	B	G	S
R	E	C	E	P	T	I	O	N	I	S	T
O	P	O	S	B	T	C	Y	M	K	O	Z
I	D	O	C	T	O	R	H	B	R	D	D
E	G	K	S	Q	P	U	J	G	F	E	W

1 ....   3 ....   5 ....   7 ....

2 ....   4 ....   6 ....   8 ....

c〉 *What do they do? Match the sentence halves.*

1   A doctor   a) flies a plane.
2   A cook   b) takes pictures.
3   A photographer   c) helps sick people.
4   A mechanic   d) visits places in different countries.
5   A pilot   e) repairs cars.
6   A driver   f) helps people in a hotel.
7   A tourist   g) prepares food.
8   A receptionist   h) drives a car or bus.

4〉 *Do the exam task. Use the clues to help you.*

Part 1

Questions 1 – 5

Who are these notices for?
For questions 1 – 5, mark A, B or C on the answer sheet.

EXAMPLE		ANSWER
0 *Free ice cream with every meal!*	A people in a bank B people in a café C people in a museum	**B**

1 **Wash hands before preparing food**	A cooks B hotel guests C cleaners	
2 WE TAKE ALL MAJOR CREDIT CARDS	A shop assistants B receptionists C tourists	
3 DO NOT CROSS WHEN LIGHT IS RED	A people in a disco B people in a plane C people walking	
4 Petrol available 24 hours	A car drivers B mechanics C bus passengers	
5 Take two tablets after eating	A doctors B hungry people C ill people	

CLUES

Question 1: Who prepares the food?

Question 2: Shop assistants and receptionists take credit cards but **who** is the notice **for**?

Question 3: Where can you see this sign? In a street? **Who** is it **for**?

Question 4: Who needs petrol?

Question 5: When do we need to *take tablets*?

PREPARATION

Part 1 – signs

- For **questions 6–10**, you read signs and notices which you might see in Britain.
- You match each sign to the correct explanation.
- There are five explanations, but eight signs.

1 〉 Read the instructions to the exam task opposite.

1 What question do you have to answer?
2 How many questions are there?
3 Where do you mark your answers in the exam?

2 〉 Look at the example 0. Why is H the right answer?

Underline the word in the explanation that means the same as LITTER in the sign.

3 〉 Grammar focus: should/shouldn't

The verbs *should/shouldn't* sometimes appear in explanations about signs.

Examples:
CHILDREN CROSSING = You **should** drive carefully.
PLEASE DO NOT PARK IN FRONT OF GARAGE = You **shouldn't** leave your car here.

Complete each sentence using should or shouldn't.

1 When you drive a car in the town, you .... drive slowly.
2 Here is the emergency exit. You .... use this exit if there's a fire. You .... use the lift.
3 This toy may break easily. You .... give it to very young children.
4 Mario has hurt his arm. We .... take him to hospital.
5 You .... buy a ticket before you get on the train.

4 〉 Vocabulary focus: shopping and services

In the exam, signs are often about shopping and services.

Where can you see these signs?

in the supermarket/at the beach/on a food packet/at the airport/in a museum/
outside a restaurant/at the sports centre/at the theatre/at the shoe shop/
in the cinema

1 | Use before 19/10/04 | 6 | A three-course meal for under £6 |

2 | CHANGING ROOMS | 7 | Special offers on dog food |

3 | Tonight's show cancelled | 8 | BOATS FOR HIRE |

4 | REPAIRS WHILE YOU WAIT | 9 | QUEUE HERE FOR TICKETS |

5 | Admission free for students | 10 | CHECK IN |

5 〉 Do the exam task. Use the clues to help you.

Part 1

Questions 6 – 10

Which notice (A – H) says this (6 – 10)?
For questions 6 – 10, mark the correct letter A – H on the answer sheet.

EXAMPLE	ANSWER
0 You shouldn't drop rubbish in the street.	**H**

6   You should be careful because this will burn.

7   You shouldn't talk loudly here.

8   You pay the same but you get more.

9   You should keep this in a cool place.

10   Be careful when you cross the road.

A   **BUY 2 GET ONE FREE**

B   *Keep this shirt away from fire!*

C   **LOOK BOTH WAYS**

D   **Store in fridge after opening**

E   **Tourist Information   500m**

F   **CHEMIST'S – closed for lunch**

G   **HOSPITAL Please be quiet**

H   **KEEP BRITAIN TIDY – TAKE YOUR LITTER HOME WITH YOU**

CLUES

Question 6: Look for something which can burn.

Question 7: Find a word which means *not loud*.

Question 8: Do you have to **pay** for more?

Question 9: Where can you keep things cool?

Question 10: What should you do before you cross the road?

Part 2 – definitions

■ For **questions 11 – 15**, you match a group of topic-related words with the correct definition.

■ This part tests your vocabulary.

1 > *Read the instructions to the exam task opposite.*

1   What vocabulary topic are all the words from?
2   How many questions are there?
3   Where do you mark your answers in the exam?

2 > *Look at the example. Why is E the right answer?*

3 > *Grammar focus:* **if and when sentences**

Sentences with *if* or *when* are sometimes used in definitions.

Examples:
If you need to buy some medicine, you should go here.   chemist's
When the weather is hot, you may go here.   beach

Match the sentence halves.

1   If you want to see a film,   a) when you are ill.
2   You go to the doctor   b) put on your raincoat.
3   When you need a plane ticket,   c) you can go to the cinema.
4   If it starts to rain,   d) if your bag is stolen.
5   If animals are kept in a zoo,   e) you can buy it at the travel agent's.
6   You should go to the police station   f) they are not free to move.

4 > *Grammar focus:* **may/will/won't**

Sometimes sentences with *will* or *may* are used in definitions.

Examples:
You **will** get wet in the rain if you don't put this on.   (It's certain)   raincoat
You **may** see these in the river.   (It's possible)   fish

Read these predictions. How certain do you think they are? Complete them with **will, won't** *or* **may.**

1   Our football team .... win the Cup.
2   I .... study to be a doctor when I finish school.
3   My family .... go to the USA on holiday next summer.
4   I .... pass all my exams this term.
5   I .... go to a party this weekend.

5 > *Do the exam task. Use the clues to help you.*

Part 2

Questions 11–15

Read the descriptions (11–15) of some holiday words.
What is the correct word (A–H) for each description?
For questions 11–15, mark the correct letter A–H on the answer sheet.

EXAMPLE	ANSWER
0 If you want to travel by train, go here.	E

11 When you go away on holiday, you pack your clothes in this.	**A** airport
	B swimsuit
12 You may buy some of these on your holiday.	**C** passport
	D postcard
13 This is where you will go to catch your plane.	**E** railway station
14 If you want to take photographs, you need this.	**F** suitcase
	G camera
15 You may need this to leave the country.	**H** beach bag

CLUES

Question 11: Be careful. Two answers look possible but only **one** is right.
Question 12: Be careful. Look at the word *some*. Which word fits?

Part 3 – everyday conversations

- For **questions 16 – 20**, you complete two-line conversations by choosing **A**, **B** or **C**.
- Sometimes there is a statement followed by a response.

1 ⟩ Read the instructions to the exam task opposite.

1   How many conversations are there?
2   Where do you mark your answers in the exam?

2 ⟩ Look at the example 0. Why is A the right answer?

1   Is the speaker
    a) asking if he/she can do something?
    b) apologising for something?
    c) thanking someone?

2   When do we say 'You're welcome'?
3   When do we say 'Yes, of course'?

3 ⟩ Skills focus: functions

To find the response that matches the statement, read the statement and ask yourself:
   What is the situation? Who is speaking? Where?
   What is the speaker doing? (asking for something? apologising?, etc.)
   What kind of response does he/she need?

Examples:

Statement	Situation	Response
I'd like a pizza and a juice, please.	ordering in a restaurant	Certainly. Anything else?
I'm sorry I lost your book.	apologising to a friend	That's all right.

a ⟩ Read the conversations. Who is speaking? What is the situation?

1   A: You should go to the doctor.   B: Yes, you're right.
2   A: Well done!   B: Thanks.
3   A: I hate doing homework!   B: So do I.
4   A: Come on, let's go for a walk.   B: OK, why not?
5   A: This CD player is broken.   B: What's wrong with it?

b ⟩ What is A doing in each conversation? There are two functions you don't need.

a) complaining   ..5..   d) greeting somebody   .....   f) giving an opinion   .....

b) giving advice   .....   e) congratulating somebody .....   g) expressing good wishes   .....

c) making a suggestion .....

c ⟩ Read the conversations. The answers are in the wrong place. Write the correct response on the line.

1   A: I'd like to try on that dress, please.   a) B: Hi, how are you?   ....
2   A: Hurry up, we're late.   b) B: Thanks, I will.   ....
3   A: I feel much better now.   c) B: What size are you?   ....
4   A: This is Pablo speaking.   d) B: Good, I'm glad.   ....
5   A: Enjoy your holiday.   e) B: Sorry, I'm just coming.   ....

4 ⟩ Do the exam task. Use the clues to help you.

Part 3
Questions 16 – 20

Complete the five conversations.
For questions 16 – 20, mark A, B or C on the answer sheet.

EXAMPLE		ANSWER
0	I'm sorry I'm late. A That's all right. B Yes, of course. C You're welcome.	A

16 Let's go to the zoo tomorrow.

    A It doesn't matter.
    B What time?
    C That's a good idea.

17 Hi! This is David speaking.

    A Hello, David.
    B He's not here.
    C I'll get him for you.

18 I'd like a double room with a shower.

    A How much is that?
    B Certainly, madam.
    C Is it a quiet room?

19 Could you pass me the bread, please?

    A Why not?
    B No, thank you.
    C Here you are.

20 You really should see the dentist.

    A Yes, you're right.
    B She's Dr Caxton.
    C Are you?

CLUES

Question 16: The first speaker is **making a suggestion**. Which response fits?

Question 17: The first speaker is **greeting someone** on the phone.

Question 18: The first speaker is **booking a room** in a hotel.

Question 19: The first speaker is **asking** for the bread.

Question 20: The first speaker is **offering some advice**.

Part 3 – everyday conversations

■ For **questions 21 – 25**, you complete a longer conversation by choosing from a list of options.

■ One speaker may want to complain about something, make arrangements, ask for information, book a hotel room, buy a train ticket, etc.

1 ⟩ Read the instructions to the exam task opposite.

1 Where does the conversation take place?
2 What are the speakers called?
3 Where do you mark your answers in the exam?

2 ⟩ Look at the example 0. Why is E the right answer?

1 When you answer the phone, you usually say your name and phone number. What does the other person say then?
2 Check your answer. Read the line after the example. What does Mary say?

3 ⟩ Skills focus: choosing the right option

a ⟩ Read the gapped conversation. Then answer the questions below.

Mario: Gina, would you like to come to the concert with us on Wednesday?

Gina: 1 ....

Mario: Ben and Elena. They really like the band. What about you?

Gina: 2 ....

Mario: He plays the drums as well as the guitar, you know. Are you going to come?

Gina: 3 ....

Mario: Yes, no problem. I've got enough money to pay for all the tickets.

Gina: 4 ....

Mario: The best ones are £25 but we can get cheaper ones for £15.

Gina: 5 ....

Mario: OK, I'll get four £15 tickets.

Gina: 6 ....

1 What does Mario invite Gina to do? Does she agree immediately?
2 Who do you think Ben and Elena are?
3 Why does Mario talk about the drummer?
4 Mario says *Yes, no problem.* What do you think Gina asked him?
5 What do you think Gina asks about the tickets?
6 How many tickets is Mario going to buy?
7 Is Gina going to go to the concert?

b ⟩ What does Gina say to Mario? Choose Gina's responses from the list below. Write a) – f) on the lines 1 – 6 above.

a) They're OK. I like the guitarist! d) I can't afford the expensive ones.
b) Thanks.   e) I don't know yet. Who else is going?
c) How much do they cost?   f) All right. Can I give you the money later?

4 ⟩ Do the exam task opposite. Use the clues to help you.

Part 3

Questions 21 – 25

Complete the telephone conversation.
What does Peter say to Mary?
For questions 21 – 25, mark the correct letter A – H on the answer sheet.

EXAMPLE	ANSWER
Mary: Hello, 798301.	
Peter: **0**	**E**

Mary: Hi, Peter. Friday evening? I'm not sure yet. Why?

Peter: **21** ....

Mary: Really? That's great! Where are they playing?

Peter: **22** ....

Mary: I'd really love to come, but how much are the tickets? Are they expensive?

Peter: **23** ....

Mary: Lucky you! Will we have to leave home early?

Peter: **24** ....

Mary: What time should we meet?

Peter: **25** ....

Mary: OK, thanks very much, Peter. Goodbye.

Peter: Goodbye, Mary.

A They're free! I won them in that competition at college.

B Well, I've got two tickets for the Blue Stars concert.

C Do you want my address?

D I think so. There may be a lot of traffic on the road to Oxford.

E Hi, Mary, it's Peter. Are you free on Friday evening?

F I'm not sure yet. I'll call you again on Thursday to arrange the time.

G I'm not playing.

H In Oxford, at the new concert hall.

CLUES

Question 21: Mary asks *Why?* Look for a reason.

Question 22: Mary asks *Where?* Look for a place for the concert.

Question 23: Mary wants to know if the tickets are *expensive*. What does Peter reply?

Question 24: Why might they have to leave home early?

Question 25: Mary asks a question about the time. Look for a response with the time in it.

Part 4 – factual text

■ For **questions 26 – 32**, you read a short text (about 200 words).

■ You answer questions about it. Sometimes you have to decide if a statement is Right or Wrong.

1 ⟩ **Look at the instructions and the title of the text opposite.**

1 What is the text about?
2 What do you have to do in this task?
3 Where do you mark your answers in the exam?

2 ⟩ **Look at the words in the box. Which words do you think are in the text? Choose five and tick ✔ them.**

homework   goal   club   football boots   team   school   game   champion

3 ⟩ **Look through the text quickly. Check your answers to exercise 2. Were you right?**

4 ⟩ **Read the text carefully. Answer these questions. <u>Underline</u> the answers in the text.**

1 Who is the youngest player in the team?
2 Who won the competition?
3 How old is Jamie?
4 Why is Jamie happy and excited?
5 How long has Jamie played football?
6 When did Jamie score his first goal?
7 How much time does Jamie spend with Manchester United?
8 Where does Jamie have his school lessons?
9 When does Jamie see his friends?

5 ⟩ **Look at the example 0. Why is A the right answer?**

1 What do you know about Jamie's age?
2 Why aren't **B** or **C** possible?

6 ⟩ **Read the questions and do the exam task. Use the clues to help you.**

CLUES

Question 26: Who *won* the competition? So who plays for Manchester United?

Question 27: Jamie is *very* young but is he too young to play?

Question 28: Find a word which means *pleased* in the text.

Question 29: Think of a different way to say *at the age of six*.

Question 30: Can you find anything in the text about *every day of the week*?

Question 31: Jamie doesn't go to school but does he *miss* anything from school?

Question 32: Can you find any information in the text about Jamie seeing his friends during the week?

Part 4

Questions 26 – 32

Read the article about a young boy who wants to be a footballer.
Are sentences 26 – 32 'Right' (A) or 'Wrong' (B)?
If there is not enough information to answer 'Right' (A) or 'Wrong' (B), choose 'Doesn't say' (C).
For questions 26 – 32, mark A, B or C on the answer sheet.

A new young player

For our interview this week, we talked to Jamie Zvenison, the newest and youngest football player with the Manchester United Young Players team. Jamie was in a football skills competition with fifteen other young players and he was the winner!

Jamie is still very young, only sixteen, but now he's going to play for Manchester United. He told me that he feels very happy and excited about this because he has always dreamed of playing football for a famous club. He has played football all his life and he remembers scoring his first goal at school when he was only six years old!

Because Jamie has to spend a lot of time with the Manchester United Young Players team, he can't go to school. Lucky him! But the club makes sure he continues his lessons with a teacher at his home so Jamie does not miss anything from school, including homework!

Jamie is able to phone his friends every day and sometimes he sends them an email. He can't see them as much as he wants to but they often come to watch him play football for the Manchester United Young Players team at weekends.

EXAMPLE			ANSWER
0 There is nobody younger than Jamie in the team.			
A Right	**B** Wrong	**C** Doesn't say	**A**

---

26 All the players in the competition now play for Manchester United.
  A Right **B** Wrong **C** Doesn't say

27 Jamie is too young to play for Manchester United.
  A Right **B** Wrong **C** Doesn't say

28 Jamie is pleased about playing for Manchester United.
  A Right **B** Wrong **C** Doesn't say

29 Jamie scored his first goal at the age of six.
  A Right **B** Wrong **C** Doesn't say

30 Jamie is with the team every day of the week.
  A Right **B** Wrong **C** Doesn't say

31 Jamie doesn't have to do any school work.
  A Right **B** Wrong **C** Doesn't say

32 Jamie sometimes sees his friends during the week.
  A Right **B** Wrong **C** Doesn't say

Part 5 – gapped text

- For **questions 33 – 40**, you read a short factual text with eight numbered spaces.
- You choose **one** word **A**, **B** or **C** to fill each space.
- This part tests your grammar.

1 〉 Read the instructions and the title of the text opposite.

1   What is the text about?
2   How many questions are there?
3   Where do you mark your answers in the exam?

2 〉 Look at the example 0. Why is B the correct answer?

1   The sentence compares different types of shark. We use *most* to make the superlative form of long adjectives.
2   Look at **A** and **C**. Can we use these words in a comparison?

3 〉 *Grammar focus:* comparatives and superlatives

This part often tests comparisons (e.g. *smaller than*) and superlatives (e.g. *the smallest*).

a 〉 Complete the table. Write in the missing words.

Adjective	Comparative	Superlative
....	....	the longest
....	bigger	....
dirty	....	....
....	more dangerous	....
....	better	....
....	worse	....

b 〉 Complete each sentence with the correct adjective form.

1   A white whale is .... (heavy) than a shark.
2   The cheetah is the .... (fast) animal on the planet.
3   The hummingbird is one of the .... (beautiful) birds in the world.
4   Pollution in the sea is now much .... (bad) than it was.
5   Studying animals is much .... (good) than studying maths!

c 〉 Make comparisons as in the example.

1   whale / gorilla – endangered.   The whale is not as endangered as the gorilla. ....
2   tiger / dolphin – intelligent   ....
3   whales / sharks – dangerous   ....
4   lions / cheetahs – fast   ....
5   rhino / elephant – heavy   ....

4 〉 Do the exam task. Use the clues to help you.

Part 5

Questions 33 – 40

Read the article about the sharks and whales.
Choose the best word (A, B or C) for each space (33 – 40).
For questions 33 – 40, mark A, B or C on the answer sheet.

SHARKS AND WHALES

There are many different types of shark but the ____**0**____ famous of all is the Great White Shark. Some ____**33**____ these sharks weigh nearly two thousand kilos and can be six metres ____**34**____ . However, the Blue Whale is much ____**35**____ . It can weigh as much ____**36**____ thirteen thousand kilos and is often more ____**37**____ thirty metres long.

Although the Blue Whale is so big, ____**38**____ is much less dangerous than the Great White Shark. The Great White is the most dangerous thing in the sea. It finds its food close ____**39**____ beaches where the water is not too deep and has killed people swimming in the sea. A Great White Shark's stomach ____**40**____ often bigger than a human adult.

EXAMPLE			ANSWER
0 A too	**B** most	**C** very	**B**

33	**A** of	**B** from	**C** for
34	**A** long	**B** tall	**C** high
35	**A** big	**B** bigger	**C** biggest
36	**A** to	**B** for	**C** as
37	**A** than	**B** that	**C** and
38	**A** he	**B** it	**C** they
39	**A** on	**B** to	**C** at
40	**A** is	**B** are	**C** be

CLUES

Question 33: Which preposition do we often use after *some*?

Question 34: Think about the **shape** of the shark.

Question 35: Which adjective form can you use after *much*?

Question 36: Look at the expression *as much ...* . What is missing?

Question 37: *More* is often followed by ...?

Question 38: You need a pronoun here. What is the subject of the sentence?

Question 39: Which preposition do you need after *close*?

Question 40: Which verb form do you need?

Part 6 – gapped letter/note

- For **questions 41–50**, you read a short text with ten numbered spaces.
- You have to think of **one** word for each space.
- You must spell the words correctly.
- This part tests your grammar and vocabulary.

1 ⟩ *Read the instructions to the exam task opposite.*

1 How many letters are there?
2 How many questions are there?
3 Where do you mark your answers in the exam?

2 ⟩ *Grammar focus: -ing and to infinitive*

This part may test verb forms.
- We use the *-ing* form after some verbs, e.g.:
  I like/love/hate/don't mind study**ing** English.
- We use the *to* infinitive form after some verbs and adjectives, e.g.:
  I hope/want/would like **to visit** London soon.
  I was pleased **to get** a letter from my friend.

Put the verbs in brackets into the correct form.

1 I like .... (learn) languages at school.
2 I would like .... (work) in another country.
3 Are you planning .... (visit) me next week?
4 Last night we decided .... (go) to the cinema.
5 I will be happy .... (come) to your party next week.

3 ⟩ *Read the letter and the reply. Then underline the correct word in each pair.*

Dear Maria,

Are you studying very hard? Please write to me **(1) when/as** you've got time. I would like **(2) to know/knowing** if you are coming **(3) to stay/staying** with me next week. Remember it's **(4) my/mine** birthday and I'm planning **(5) to have/having** a party on Saturday!

Love,
Carlo

Dear Carlo,

Yes, I'm doing a lot of **(6) study/studying**! Don't worry, I'm coming to **(7) you/your** house next week **(8) with/for** the party. What time does **(9) it/its** start? Do you want me **(10) to bring/bringing** something? Is it alright **(11) to stay/staying** for two nights? There **(12) is/are** no trains on Sunday.

Love,
Maria

4 ⟩ *Read the texts opposite quickly.*

1 Who is the first letter from? Who is it to?
2 What is the reason for writing?
3 Who is the second letter from? Who is it to?
4 What is the reason for writing?

5 ⟩ *Do the exam task. Read each sentence and decide what kind of word goes in the space. Use the clues to help you.*

Part 6

Questions 41 – 50

Complete these letters.
Write ONE word in each space (41 – 50).
For questions 41 – 50, write your words on the answer sheet.

London English School
109 Bath Street
London NW25 9JH
20th November

Dear Sir,

I'm (**Example:** _writing_) to thank you
_____41_____ the tourist information which
you sent. My students enjoyed reading
everything. Some of _____42_____ are
planning _____43_____ visit Cardiff soon.
I _____44_____ sure they will have _____45_____
good time.

Yours,

Matthew Martins

Tourist Information Office
39 Chester Road
Cardiff CA23 7YH
28th November

Dear Mr Martins,

I _____46_____ very happy to _____47_____ your
letter. We send information to thousands
of people _____48_____ year and many choose
to visit Wales. I hope that your students
enjoy _____49_____ trip. Please telephone me
_____50_____ you need any more help.

Yours sincerely,

Jason Brown

CLUES

Question 41: You need a preposition here.

Question 42: You need a pronoun which means *my students*.

Question 43: Which verb form comes after *planning*?

Question 44: Think of a verb for this space.

Question 45: What is the missing word in the phrase *have ... good time*?

Question 46: Think about **when** the writer received the letter. What tense do you need?

Question 47: Think of a verb for this space.

Question 48: How often do they send information?

Question 49: You need a pronoun: which one?

Question 50: Which word can link the parts of this sentence?

Part 7 – completing a form

- For **questions 51 – 55**, you read a short text (about 50 words).
- Then you complete a form using information from the text.
- You do not need to write sentences – only words and short phrases.
- Correct spelling and use of capital letters is essential.

1 ⟩ *Read the instructions to the exam task opposite.*

1 Who are you going to read about?
2 What kind of form do you have to fill in?

2 ⟩ *Vocabulary focus:* describing things

a ⟩ *Complete the conversation at the Lost Property Office. What does Darren say to the assistant?*

Assistant: Hello, can I help you?

Darren: 1 ....

Assistant: What does it look like?

Darren: 2 ....

Assistant: No, I'm sorry. No one has handed in a bag like that. You'll have to fill in a form.

Darren: 3 ....

Assistant: Please can you give me your name and address.

Darren: 4 ....

Assistant: Can you remember what was in your bag?

Darren: 5 ....

Assistant: And where did you lose it?

Darren: 6 ....

Assistant: OK. Come back in a day or two. Maybe you will be lucky.

A Yes, I suppose that's the best thing to do.

B On the train, I think.

C My sports shoes and shorts.

D Yes, please. I've lost my bag. Has anyone handed it in?

E I was with my sister.

F It's green and white. It's got a zip and a shoulder strap.

G It's about 60 centimetres long.

H Darren Jones, 29 Halley Street. That's H-A- double L-E-Y.

b ⟩ *Check your answers by reading the conversation with a partner.*

c ⟩ *Imagine you have lost one of your own personal possessions. With a partner, practise a similar conversation at the Lost Property Office.*

3 ⟩ *Do the exam task. Use the clues to help you.*

Part 7

Questions 51 – 55

Read the information about Belinda Brown.
Fill in the information on the Lost Property Form for her.
For questions 51 – 55, write the information on the answer sheet.

Belinda Brown has lost her sports bag. It's red and white and made of nylon, and is about 50 centimetres x 30 centimetres. Her school books are in the bag. She left it on a number 49 bus on 15th July. She got off the bus at about 8.30 a.m.

Lost Property Form

Name:	Belinda Brown
Item lost:	51
Colour:	52
Size:	53
Contents:	54
Where last seen:	55
Date lost:	15th July

CLUES

Question 51: Just write the name of the item, not a description.

Question 52: Copy the words carefully from the text.

Question 53: Write both measurements.

Question 54: This means 'What was inside the bag?'.

Part 8 – writing a note

- This part tests your writing skills.
- Sometimes you read a note from someone and you write a short reply.
- There are 3–4 different things to write about.

1⟩ Read the instructions for the writing task below.

1 What do you have to do first?
2 Underline the questions you have to reply to. How many are there?
3 How many words should you write?

Read the note from your new pen friend.
Write a note to answer his question.

> Hi Theo!
> We're going to meet at last. Where should I wait? What do you look like? What clothes will you wear?
> See you on Sunday!
> Bye,
> Daniel.

Write 20 – 25 words.
Write your note on the back of the answer sheet.

2⟩ Vocabulary focus: describing people

a⟩ Match the descriptions to the pictures.

1 Matteo is tall and slim, with long black hair and a big moustache.
2 Liz is medium-height. She has got very short, curly brown hair and a round face.
3 Peter is short and fat. He hasn't got any hair – he's bald.
4 Stella has long, straight fair hair. Her face is very long and thin and she wears glasses.

b⟩ Put the adjectives from sentences 1–4 under the correct heading. Can you add any more?

Height	Build	Hair	Face
tall			

3 > *Read the answer to the writing task in exercise 1.*

1 What information is missing?
2 Can you correct the mistakes?

Dear Daniel,

I'm medium-height, with short, curly <u>hairs</u> and I wear glasses. On Sunday, I <u>am wearing</u> blue jeans and a green <u>sweter</u>. If it <u>will be</u> cold, I will wear my brown jacket.

See you soon!
Theo

4 > *Read the exam task below.*

1 What do you have to write in this task?
2 How many things do you have to write about? <u>Underline</u> them.
3 How many words should you write?
4 Where do you write your answers in the exam?

5 > *Write your note.*

6 > *Check your writing carefully.*

- Have you answered all the questions?
- Have you written about 20 – 25 (maximum 30) words?
- Have you signed your note?
- Is your spelling correct?
- Have you used capital letters for names, etc.?

EXAM PRACTICE

Part 8

Question 56

Read the note from your friend Sara.
Write a note to answer her questions.

Hi Emily,
Thank you for asking your brother to meet me at the bus station tomorrow. What does he look like? What clothes will he wear? Where will he wait for me?
See you soon!
Sara

Write 20 – 25 words.
Write your note on the back of the answer sheet.

PAPER 2　Listening　(approximately 25 minutes)

Part 1 – five short dialogues

- For **questions 1 – 5**, you hear five short conversations.
- The conversations are between friends or relatives, or take place in a shop, at a ticket office, etc.
- You listen and choose the correct picture **A**, **B** or **C**.

In this part there are often questions about where things and people are.

1 〉 *Vocabulary focus:* location

a〉 *Look at the map. <u>Underline</u> the correct word or phrase in these sentences.*

1　The sports centre is *next to/opposite* the library.
2　There is a car park *in front of/behind* the railway station.
3　The Seafresh fish and chip shop is *opposite/on the corner of* Market Street and High Street.
4　There is a cinema *next to/between* the Tourist Information Office and the library.

b〉 📼 *Find the people on the map. Listen to the recording. Write the correct name next to each person.*

Paul/Sam/Lucy/Michael/Francesca/Mandy

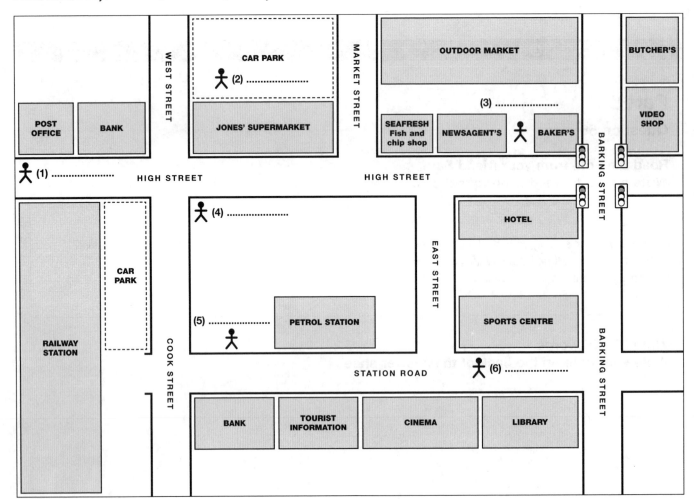

2 〉 *Communication focus:* understanding directions

a 〉 *Read the conversations and look at the map. Where do the people want to go?*

1 **Michael:** Can you tell me where the ………. is, please?

   Passerby: Yes, go straight up the road. It's on the right, opposite the sports centre.

2 **Sam:**   Where's the nearest ………. , please?

   Passerby: Go along High Street. At the traffic lights, turn left into Barking Street.
   It's on the right hand side, next to the butcher's.

3 **Mandy:**   Can you tell me the way to the ………. , please?

   Passerby: Go straight down here. Take the first turning on your right. You will see
   it in front of you at the end of the street.

b 〉 ▭ *Listen and check.*

c 〉 *Ask a partner for directions:*

1 from the bank to the library.
2 from the railway station to the hotel.

3 〉 *Communication focus:* asking for and expressing opinions

a 〉 ▭ *Read and listen to the conversations. <u>Underline</u> the words and phrases
        which ask for and express opinions.*

1 **A:** Hi, how are you?
   B: Fine. Where have you been?
   A: I've been to see the new Brad Pitt film.
   B: I saw that last week. <u>What did you think of it?</u>
   A: I thought it was fantastic. What about you?
   B: I don't agree. I didn't like it.

2 **A:** I want to buy a new CD. Who do you like best, Robbie Williams or REM?
   B: I don't like REM at all. I think their songs are terrible.
   A: Do you think so? I like them a lot. I think they're really great.
   B: I don't agree. I think Robbie Williams is much better. His new CD is brilliant.
   A: Yes, he's really good.

b 〉 *Complete the conversation. Use expressions from a* 〉*.*

A: Hello Sonia, this is Fiona. How are things?

B: Hi, Fiona. I've just finished that book you lent me.

A: The murder story? …………………… ?

B: …………………… . What …………………… ?

A: I agree. I …………………… , but my sister thought …………………… .

4 〉 ▣ *Read and listen to the instructions to the exam task below.*

1 How many conversations are there?
2 How many pictures are there for each conversation?
3 How many times will you hear each conversation?
4 How do you mark your answers?

5 〉 ▣ *Look at the example and listen to the recording.*

1 What is the question?
2 What is the answer?
3 How do you know?

6 〉 ▣ *Listen to the rest of the recording and answer questions 1 – 5.*

EXAM PRACTICE

Part 1
Questions 1 – 5

Listen to the tape.
You will hear five short conversations.
You will hear each conversation twice.
There is one question for each conversation.
For questions 1 – 5, put a tick ✔ under the right answer.

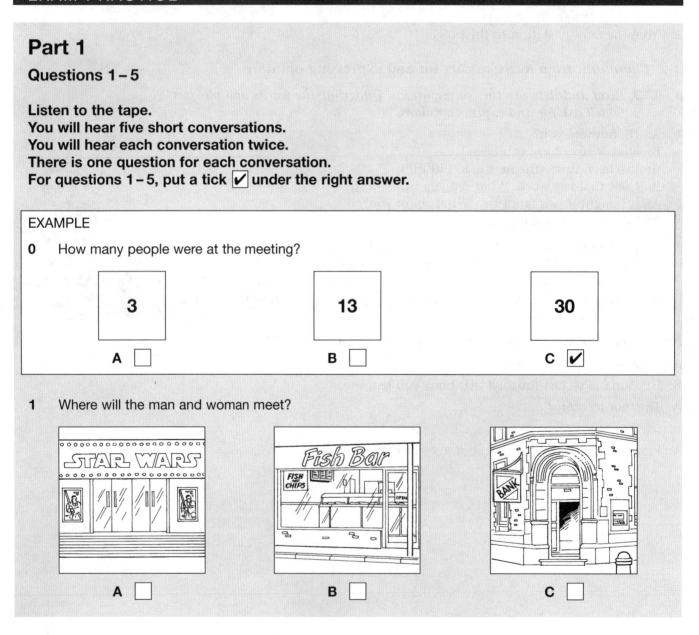

EXAMPLE

0 How many people were at the meeting?

3	13	30
A ☐	B ☐	C ✔

1 Where will the man and woman meet?

A ☐   B ☐   C ☐

2   Which picture does the man like the most?

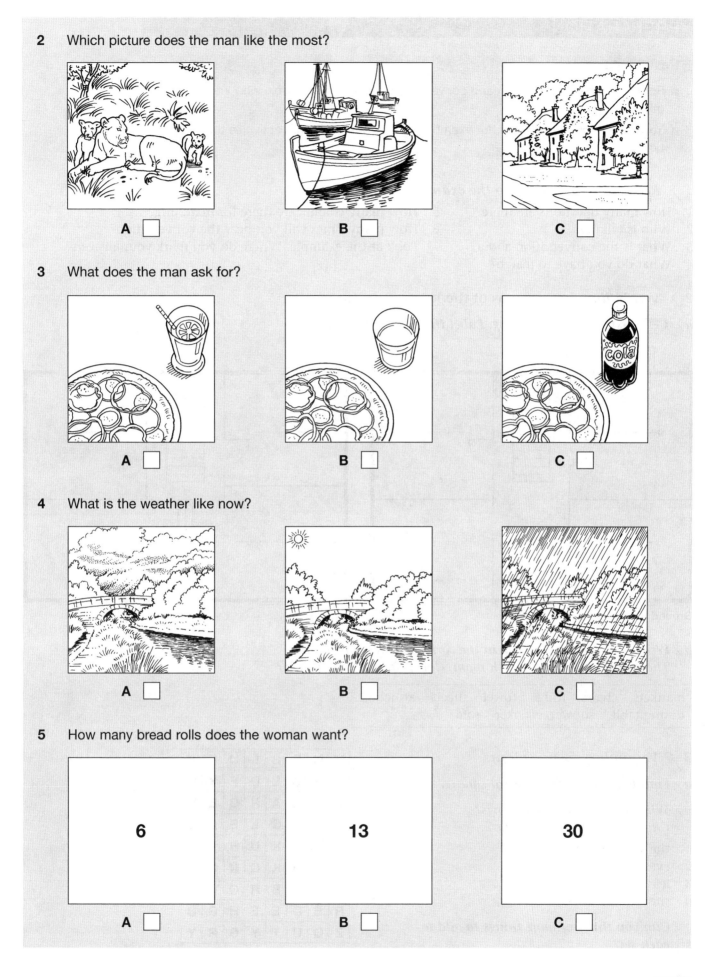

A ☐   B ☐   C ☐

3   What does the man ask for?

A ☐   B ☐   C ☐

4   What is the weather like now?

A ☐   B ☐   C ☐

5   How many bread rolls does the woman want?

6

13

30

A ☐   B ☐   C ☐

Part 2 – conversation

- For **questions 6 – 10**, you hear a conversation between two people who know each other.
- You have to match two lists, for example, names of people with activities they like doing.

1 ⟩ *Read the instructions to the exam task opposite.*

1 How many questions are there?
2 Who is talking?
3 What is the conversation about?
4 What do you have to match?

5 How many colours are there for matching?
6 How many times will you hear the conversation?
7 Look at the example. Where do you mark your answers?

2 ⟩ *Vocabulary focus: rooms of the house/furniture*

a ⟩ 🔊 *Listen to the recording. Label the rooms of the house.*

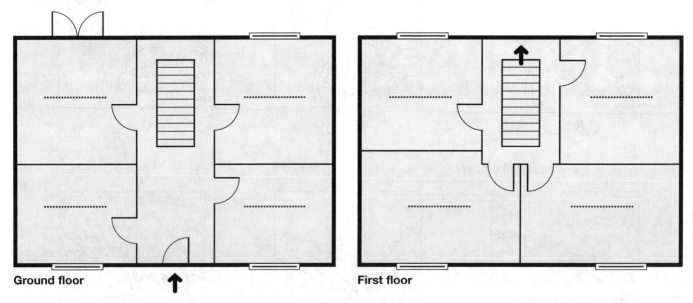

Ground floor   **First floor**

b ⟩ *Write the words in the box in the correct room of the house.*
There are two items for each room. Can you add more things?

blankets   chairs   fridge   towel   sheets   armchair
dining table   shower   cooker   sofa

3 ⟩ *Vocabulary focus: colours*

a ⟩ *Find ten colours in the word square.*

b ⟩ *What colours are these things?*
Choose from the word square.

1 the sky, the sea
2 eyes, hair
3 leaves in autumn
4 snow and ice

Can you think of more things to add to each set?

M	N	B	B	L	U	E	V
A	S	G	L	D	F	Y	G
J	O	R	A	N	G	E	H
K	W	E	C	L	E	L	O
S	H	E	K	U	B	L	S
P	I	N	K	G	N	O	M
C	T	X	B	R	O	W	N
R	E	D	E	E	H	G	B
Z	Q	U	I	Y	G	R	Y

4 〉 [cassette] *Now do the exam task. Answer questions 6–10.*

5 〉 *Compare your answers with other students. Are they the same?*

6 〉 [cassette] *Listen again. Check your answers with other students.*
Add any that you missed the first time.

EXAM PRACTICE

Part 2
Questions 6 – 10

Listen to Guilia talking to Franco about her parents' house.
They are painting the rooms.
What colour is each room?

For questions 6 – 10, write a letter A – H next to each room.
You will hear the conversation twice.

EXAMPLE	
0 bathroom	A

ROOMS		COLOURS	
6 bedroom	☐	A blue	
7 kitchen	☐	B brown	
8 study	☐	C green	
9 dining room	☐	D orange	
10 living room	☐	E pink	
		F red	
		G white	
		H yellow	

Part 3 – conversation

■ For **questions 11–15**, you hear a conversation between two people.

■ The people sometimes know each other.

■ You have to answer five questions by choosing **A**, **B** or **C**.

1〉 *Read the instructions to the exam task opposite.*

1   Who is talking?
2   What is the conversation about?
3   How do you mark your answers?
4   How many times do you hear the conversation?

2〉 ▭ *Do the exam task. Listen to the recording and answer questions 11–15.*

3〉 *Compare your answers with other students. Are they the same?*

4〉 ▭ *Listen again. Check your answers. Add any that you missed the first time.*

5〉 *Communication:* making plans

a〉 *Complete the dialogue with phrases from the box. Try to use each phrase once.*

Why don't we   I'd rather   Let's   Do you want   What about   Shall we

A: Hey, Andreas. .... going to the cinema this evening? *Star Wars* is on.

B: But it doesn't start until 10.00. .... go to the Sound Hut instead.

A: OK, that's fine by me. Oh, it's closed this week! .... go for something to eat?

B: Good idea! .... try Pizza Roma?

A: Fine. .... to go by bike or by bus?

B: .... go by bus. It's quicker.

A: OK. Fine.

b〉 ▭ *Listen and compare your answers.*

c〉 *In pairs or groups, use the information in the newspaper to plan your evening.*

Eating out

PIZZA ROMA – great pizza, ice cream and drinks, for all the family!

BURGER GIANT How much can you eat?! The best burgers and fries in town.

Cinema

PLAZA – *Friends and Enemies*, 3.00, 6.00 & 9.00. Tickets £5.50.

CINESCREEN – *Catch a Train*, 4.30 & 7.00. *Star Wars*, 10.00. Tickets £5.90.

Music

SOUND HUT – closed

JO-JO'S DISCO Doors open 8.30 p.m.

River trips

Boats leave every 45 minutes. First boat 8.30 a.m. Last boat 18.15 a.m. Two-hour trip. Tickets £3.50 single, £5.50 return.

Part 3

Questions 11–15

Listen to Jane talking to her friend Marian about her American cousins.

For questions 11–15, tick ✔ A, B or C.
You will hear the conversation twice.

EXAMPLE

0 Jane's cousins are from

A the UK. ☐

B Italy. ☐

C America. ✔

---

11 Jane's cousins will arrive on

A Sunday. ☐

B Monday. ☐

C Tuesday. ☐

12 The best thing at Pizza Roma is

A pizza. ☐

B coffee. ☐

C ice cream. ☐

13 The film they will see at the cinema is

A *Friends and Enemies.* ☐

B *Catch a Train.* ☐

C *Purple Rain.* ☐

14 The first boat leaves at

A 1.30. ☐

B 11.30. ☐

C 8.30. ☐

15 They decide to go to the beach

A by train. ☐

B by bicycle. ☐

C by bus. ☐

Part 4 – conversation

■ For **questions 16 – 20**, you hear a conversation.

■ Conversations often take place in shops, offices, etc.

■ You listen and write down missing information in a message or notes.

■ You write one or two words or numbers.

■ Spelling is not tested but you should spell simple words correctly.

1 ⟩ Read the instructions to the exam task opposite.

1   How many questions are there?

2   Who are you going to hear?

3   What are the speakers going to talk about?

4   Where do you write your answers?

5   How many times will you hear the conversation?

2 ⟩ Vocabulary focus: parts of the body

Read the descriptions of some parts of the body. What is the name of each part of the body?

1   You hear with these.   ....

2   You smell things with this.   ....

3   This joins your hand and your arm.   ....

4   Your food goes here first when you eat.   ....

5   This joins your leg and your foot.   ....

6   You have these in your mouth. You use them to bite food.   ....

3 ⟩ Vocabulary focus: health

a ⟩ Unjumble the letters to find out what's wrong.

1   Susan's got a PUTMERETAER.

....

2   Mario's got a CHAHADEE.

....

3   Christine is at home because she's got a bad OOEATHTHC.

....

4   Alison has got a terrible HGOUC.

....

5   Joe can't go out today. He's got a NAPI in his chest.

....

b ⟩ What should each person in a ⟩ do?

1   Mario. should take an aspirin.

2   .... should go to the dentist.

3   .... should see a doctor.

4   .... should stay in bed.

5   .... should take some medicine for it.

4 ⟩ *Listen and check your answers to exercise 3.*

5 > *Look at the exam task again. What kind of information is missing in questions 16 – 20?*

6 > ⬛ *Do the task. Check and complete your answers the second time you listen.*

7 > *Check your answers.*

1   How many words did you write in each space?
2   Is the spelling correct?

EXAM PRACTICE

Part 4

Questions 16 – 20

You will hear a woman talking to a doctor about how she is feeling.

Listen and complete questions 16 – 20.
You will hear the conversation twice.

INFORMATION

Doctor's name:	Dr Jenkins
Name of medicine:	**16**
To be taken:	**17** .... times a day
To be taken after:	**18**
To be taken for:	**19** .... days
Date of next appointment:	**20**

Part 5 – factual monologue

- For **questions 21 – 25**, you hear a monologue.
- The monologue is often a recorded telephone message.
- You listen and fill in missing information in a message or notes.
- You write one or two words or numbers.
- Spelling is not tested but you should spell simple words correctly.

1 ⟩ *Read the instructions to the exam task opposite.*

1 How many questions are there?
2 What are you going to hear?
3 Where do you write your answers?
4 How many times will you hear the information?

2 ⟩ *Read the notes. What kind of information is missing?*

3 ⟩ *Vocabulary focus:* sports

a ⟩ *Label each picture with the name of the sport.*

1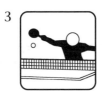
3
5
7

....

2
4
6
8

....

b ⟩ *Write the sports in* a ⟩ *under the correct heading.*

ball games		water sports	adventure sports	other individual sports
individual	team			

c ⟩ *Read the conversations and* <u>underline</u> *the verbs. Then ask and answer similar questions about other sports you know.*

1 **A:** Do you play ice hockey?   **B:** No, I don't, but I watch it on TV.
2 **A:** Have you ever gone climbing?   **B:** No, I haven't, it's very dangerous.
3 **A:** Would you like to do judo?   **B:** Yes, I think it would be interesting.

d ⟩ *Ask and answer.*

1 What is your favourite sport?
2 What sport did you play last weekend?
3 What sports have you played this week?

4 > *Vocabulary focus:* definitions

Read the descriptions of some sports. What is the name of each sport?

1   You need a table for this game.   ....
2   You need skates and a stick for this sport.   ....
3   People wear loose white trousers and a jacket when they do this.   ....
4   You do this on rivers or the sea.   ....
5   Russia has won many medals for this sport at the Olympics.   ....

5 > ▭ *Listen to the recording and do the exam task. Check and complete your answers the second time you listen.*

6 > *Check your answers.*

1   How many words did you write in each space?   2   Is the spelling correct?

EXAM PRACTICE

Part 5

Questions 21 – 25

You will hear some information about a sports centre.

Listen and complete questions 21 – 25.
You will hear the information twice.

CAMBRIDGE SPORTS CENTRE

Monday–Friday opening hours:	8.00 a.m. to 10.00 p.m.
Weekend opening hours:	**21** _____ to _____
Sports include:	**22** basketball, tennis and _____
Six-month season ticket costs:	**23** £ _____
Special gift:	T-shirt
Centre reopens on:	**24** Monday _____
New telephone number:	**25** Cambridge _____

You now have eight minutes to write your answers on the answer sheet.

PAPER 3 Speaking (8 – 10 minutes)

PREPARATION

Part 1 – personal, factual information

- This part is 5 – 6 minutes.
- You will probably be with one other candidate.
- One examiner asks you some questions. The other listens.
- You should be able to:
  - talk about where you come from and what you do (job or studies).
  - answer general personal questions, e.g. about family and friends.
  - answer questions about your daily life, interests and likes.

1 〉 Giving personal information

a 〉 🔲 *Look at the questions and answers. Listen and tick the answer you hear.*

Examiner: What do you think of your home town?
Candidate: a) I love it. It's small and friendly.
　　　　　　　b) It's OK. There's not much to do there.
Examiner: Which other towns have you visited in your country?
Candidate: a) I've been to the capital with my family.
　　　　　　　b) I've been to lots of other towns.
Examiner: Have you travelled to another country?
Candidate: a) No, I haven't, but I'd like to.
　　　　　　　b) Yes, I've been to Britain for a holiday with my family.
Examiner: Which country would you like to visit?
Candidate: a) Australia. I'd like to see a kangaroo.
　　　　　　　b) The USA. I think it's a very interesting country.

b 〉 *Ask and answer the questions with a partner. Give answers about yourself.*

2 〉 Talking about past and future activities

a 〉 *Look at the questions and answers. Complete the answers by putting the verb into the correct form.*

Examiner: What did you do last weekend?

Candidate: I .... (have) a party and all my friends .... (come).

Examiner: Did you enjoy yourself?

Candidate: Yes, we .... (dance) and everyone .... (have) a great time.

Examiner: Did you go away on holiday last year?

Candidate: Yes, my family .... (stay) in a villa by the seaside.

Examiner: What did you do on holiday?

Candidate: I .... (go) swimming every day. And I .... (do) some sightseeing in the town.

Examiner: What are you going to do next weekend?

Candidate: My friends and I .... (go) to the funfair in the park.

Examiner: Do you have any plans for the future?

Candidate: Yes, I want .... (be) a doctor.

b 〉 🔲 *Listen and check your answers.*

c 〉 *Ask and answer the questions with a partner. Give answers about yourself.*

Part 1

> 📼 **Work with a partner. Listen to the tape. You will hear an examiner asking some questions.**
> **Student A: Listen carefully and answer your questions. Tell your partner the answers.**
> **Student B: Listen carefully and answer your questions. Tell your partner the answers.**

PREPARATION

Part 2 – prompt card activity

- This part lasts 3 – 4 minutes.
- You have to make five questions and ask your partner.
- Then you have to answer your partner's questions.
- The examiners will just listen to you.
- The questions may be about personal information.

1 〉 *Look at the example exam task and the prompt card on page 78.*

Answer the questions.

1   What information is candidate A given?
2   Does candidate B have this information?
3   What does candidate B have to do?
4   Do you have to write anything?

A, here is some information about **a museum**.

CHILDREN'S MUSEUM

Over 5,000 toys to look at!

Open every day 9.00 a.m. – 4.30 p.m.

Café – drinks and snacks

Car park – 50p

Entrance: adults £2.50, children free
Wednesday only – special price for students £1.00!

B, you don't know anything about **the museum** so ask **A** some questions about it. Now, **B**, ask **A** your questions about **the museum** and **A**, you answer them.

CHILDREN'S MUSEUM

♦ what / see?

♦ open / Sundays?

♦ food / drink?

♦ how /get there?

♦ ticket / £?

---

2 ⟩ *Grammar focus:* **making questions**

a ⟩ *Put the jumbled words in the right order to make questions.*

1   you Museum at can the Children's see What ?

....

2   it Sundays open Is on ?

....

3   eat anything and buy there Can to you drink ?

....

4   I get How can there ?

....

5   it does much cost How ?

....

b ⟩ 🔲 *Listen and check your answers.*

c ⟩ *Take turns to ask and answer the questions with a partner. Use the information on page 77 to help you answer.*

3 ⟩ *Now do the exam tasks on the next page.*

Part 2

Candidate A

A, here is some information about **a shop which sells CDs**. (Turn to page 122.)

B, you don't know anything about **the shop** so ask **A** some questions about it.

Use these words to help you.

CD MARKET

◆ address?

◆ large / small?

◆ closed / Saturdays?

◆ kind of music?

◆ telephone number?

Do you understand?

Now **B**, ask **A** your questions about **the CD shop** and **A**, you answer them.

Candidate B

B, here is some information about **a youth club**. (Turn to page 126.)

A, you don't know anything about **the club** so ask **B** some questions about it.

Use these words to help you.

YOUTH CLUB

◆ who / for?

◆ days open?

◆ cost? £?

◆ what / do?

◆ where?

Do you understand?

Now **A**, ask **B** your questions about **the club** and **B**, you answer them.

TESTS 3-4

Tests 3 and 4 give you the opportunity to practise what you have learned in Tests 1 and 2.

Test 3 contains exam **Tips!** to help you with each task.

You can use these tests for timed practice, so you get used to doing the tasks under exam conditions.

When you have finished, you will be able to take the exam with confidence.

Good luck!

TEST 3

PAPER 1   Reading and Writing   (1 hour 10 minutes)

Part 1

Questions 1–5

Where can you see these notices?
For questions 1–5, mark A, B or C on the answer sheet.

EXAMPLE		ANSWER
0	**Please DO NOT feed the animals**	A in a station
		B in a café **C**
		C in a zoo

 Tip! ≫ *Think carefully about the meaning of the notices. Remember, the question asks 'Where can you see these notices?'.*

1   **Today's TV inside on page 9**

    A   on the radio

    B   in a newspaper

    C   in a book

2   **HAND WASH ONLY – 40°C**

    A   on a sweater

    B   on a washing machine

    C   in a bathroom

3   **TICKETS HERE**

    A   in a café

    B   on a plane

    C   at a railway station

4   **Push to open**

    A   on a door

    B   on a light

    C   on a present

5   **Phone 2491 8076 for film times and seat prices**

    A   outside a video shop

    B   on a bus

    C   at a cinema

[Turn over

Questions 6 – 10

Which notice (A – H) says this (6 – 10)?
For questions 6 – 10, mark the correct letter A – H on the answer sheet.

EXAMPLE	ANSWER
0 You can't smoke here.	**H**

 There are always two extra choices which you do not need to use. Make sure you look at all the choices before you choose your answer.

6   People do not eat this.

A
> No entry to
> swimming pool
> after 7 p.m.

7   Car drivers can only use this road in the day.

B
> Call 798 0891
> for details

8   If you phone this number, you will get more information.

C
> OPEN 24 HOURS

9   You can get out from here.

D
> Bird food.
> Only 75p a bag

10   People can go here all night.

E
> Restaurant
> opens at 11 a.m.

F
> ROAD CLOSED
> 10 p.m. – 6 a.m.

G
> EXIT

H
> No smoking

Part 2

Questions 11–15

Read the descriptions (11–15) of food and drink.
What is the name (A–H) of each one?
For questions 11–15, mark the correct letter A–H on the answer sheet.

EXAMPLE	ANSWER
0 People like this with toast and butter.	**D**

 Tip! >> *Be careful! Sometimes you may think two answers are possible but there is only one correct answer for each question.*

FOOD AND DRINK

11 Use this to make a drink colder.

   A chocolate

   B fish

12 If you eat too much of this, it is bad for your teeth.

   C ice

   D marmalade

13 Some people may put this in tea or coffee.

   E milk

   F salt

14 If you eat a salad, you may have these.

   G tomatoes

   H wine

15 You often see this on the table with the pepper.

[Turn over

Part 3

Questions 16 – 20

Complete the five conversations.
For questions 16 – 20, mark A, B or C on the answer sheet.

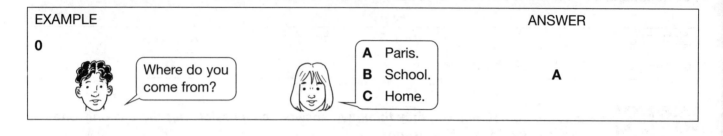

EXAMPLE		ANSWER
0	Where do you come from? A Paris. B School. C Home.	A

16 Would you check my homework, please?

    A Can I do it later?

    B Yes, let's.

    C No, you're wrong.

17 What about coming to the match with me?

    A When did you go?

    B What time does it start?

    C I haven't got one.

18 When's your birthday?

    A I'm 15 now.

    B Congratulations!

    C Tomorrow!

19 They closed the swimming pool last year.

    A Why not?

    B When does it open?

    C Did they?

20 I'm sorry I'm late.

    A That's all right.

    B Yes, of course.

    C You're welcome.

Tip! >> *After you choose your answers, say the conversations quietly to yourself. Do they make sense?*

Questions 21 – 25

Complete the conversation at the railway station.
What does the woman say to the man?
For questions 21 – 25, mark the correct letter A – H on the answer sheet.

Tip! >> *Read the whole conversation first for understanding. Then read the line before and after the gap before you choose your answers.*

EXAMPLE	ANSWER
Man: Good morning, madam. Can I help you?	
Woman: **0**	**E**

Man: Yes, madam. Do you want to travel today?

Woman: **21** ....

Man: I see. What time do you want to leave here?

Woman: **22** ....

Man: Yes, there's a fast train which leaves at twenty-five past one.

Woman: **23** ....

Man: Let me see. The express gets to London at three twenty.

Woman: **24** ....

Man: It costs thirty-three pounds eighty.

Woman: **25** ....

Man: Goodbye.

A   Well, the meeting is at four o'clock. Is there a train at about one thirty?

B   And what time does it arrive in London?

C   No, I want to travel today.

D   Thank you very much for your help. Goodbye.

E   Yes, I hope so. I need to know about trains to London.

F   Twenty past three? Good. How much is a return ticket?

G   I don't know when I want to go.

H   No, tomorrow. I have a meeting in London.

[Turn over

Part 4

Questions 26 – 32

Read the information about a school in the USA and then answer the questions.
For questions 26 – 32, mark A, B or C on the answer sheet.

Read the whole text for understanding before you look at the questions.
There may be some words you don't know, but you won't be tested on these.
Read the instructions carefully. What do you have to do?
Look for words in the text that mean the same as the questions.

BEVERLY HILLS HIGH

A school for stars

This is the school from the television show *Beverly Hills 90210*. Most of the students come from rich families and some of them have famous parents. People from Hollywood sometimes go to Beverly Hills High to look for future actors.

School life

There are lots of good things about going to this school: there are two theatres, a television studio and a radio station. The students make TV programmes and films in their drama classes. The biggest event of the school year is the school dance, or 'prom'. Everyone at Beverly Hills High travels to the prom in a limousine!

Travelling to school

In California, children can learn to drive three months before their sixteenth birthday. Lots of students at Beverly Hills High have their own cars but they have to pay a lot of money to park their cars in the school car park.

What the kids think

Most kids enjoy going to Beverly Hills High because it is fun and there is lots to do. But some kids do not like the school if their parents don't have enough money to buy them a fast car and expensive clothes.

(Adapted from 'Beverly Hills High' published in *Crown* 1st September/October 2001 pages 10 – 11 © Mary Glasgow Magazines/Scholastic.)

EXAMPLE	ANSWER
0 *Beverly Hills 90210* is. **A** a school. **B** a TV show. **C** a club.	**B**

26 The students are usually

   A   actors.   **B**   rich.   **C**   famous.

27 Beverly Hills High doesn't have

   A   a radio station.   **B**   a cinema.   **C**   a TV studio.

28 In drama classes students

   A   make radio programmes.   **B**   do dance shows.   **C**   make TV programmes.

29 The prom is

   A   a dance.   **B**   a TV programme.   **C**   a limousine.

30 In California, children can learn to drive

   A   when they are 16.   **B**   before they are 16.   **C**   after they are 16.

31 At Beverly Hills High, car parking

   A   is expensive.   **B**   is free.   **C**   is cheap.

32 Some kids don't like going to Beverly Hills High because

   A   it isn't fun.   **B**   they haven't got a fast car.   **C**   there's nothing to do.

[Turn over

Part 5

Questions 33 – 40

Read the article about tennis.
Choose the best word (A, B or C) for each space (33 – 40).
For questions 33 – 40, mark A, B or C on the answer sheet.

 Read the whole text for understanding before you look at the words.
Write your choices in the spaces. Then read the whole text again. Does it make sense?

TENNIS

You may never be the best player in the world but ___**0**___ you enjoy tennis and want to get better, read this!

First, find a teacher who can train you ___**33**___ give you some exercises to do. Make sure it is someone you like! Next, try ___**34**___ play for your school team ___**35**___ a club in the town where you live. This will give you lots of practice.

When you are ready, your teacher ___**36**___ enter you for a competition. This may be in ___**37**___ home town or you may have to travel ___**38**___ a different place. You will play against other tennis players who ___**39**___ like you – still learning!

If everything goes ___**40**___ , one day you may be one of the top players.

EXAMPLE			ANSWER
0 **A** now	**B** when	**C** if	**C**

33 **A** and   **B** but   **C** also

34 **A** be   **B** to   **C** for

35 **A** or   **B** but   **C** also

36 **A** did   **B** does   **C** will

37 **A** you   **B** yours   **C** your

38 **A** in   **B** to   **C** at

39 **A** are   **B** is   **C** have

40 **A** good   **B** well   **C** better

Part 6

Complete the postcard.
Write **ONE** word in each space (41 – 50).
For questions 41 – 50, write your words on the answer sheet.

Tip! >> *Remember to write only one word in each space and check your spelling very carefully!*

Dear Alvaro,

I'm having a great (**Example:** _time_) here in Spain!
The weather __41__ very good. It has __42__ very
hot every day and __43__ hasn't rained.

This morning, we __44__ to the beach for a swim.
Tomorrow we __45__ going shopping in the afternoon.
I want to buy __46__ presents to __47__ home for my
family. There's also a big castle __48__ a hill that I
want to visit.

I arrive at __49__ airport at 11.30 on Monday night.
I will phone __50__ on Tuesday morning and tell you
about my holiday.

See you soon!

Pietro

[Turn over

Part 7

Questions 51 – 55

Read the information about Giovanni.
Fill in the information on the Order Form for him.
For questions 51 – 55, write the information on the answer sheet.

 Tip! You do not have to write more than one or two words but spelling and capital letters are very important. Check your writing very carefully.

Giovanni Pelucci is from Rome and he lives at 46 via Vittoria. He plays for the football team in his town. He already has football shorts and now he wants to buy a black and white team shirt. He is 16 years old and he is not big.

ORDER FORM

First name:	Giovanni
Surname:	**51**
Address:	**52**
Shirt/Shorts?	**53**
Colours:	**54**
Small/Large?	**55**

Part 8

Question 56

 Tip! *Make sure you write answers to all the questions. Check your writing carefully for any mistakes.*

You are going to the shops.

Leave a note for your friend.

Tell him/her:

– **which** shops you are going to

– **what** you are going to buy

– **what time** you will be back

Write 20 – 25 words.
Write your note on the back of the answer sheet.

PAPER 2 Listening (approximately 25 minutes)

Part 1

Questions 1–5

 Tip! 》 *The pictures will help you, so look at them carefully. There are always three choices but only one is correct.*
Choose your answers when you listen the first time.
Check your answers when you listen the second time.

Listen to the tape.
You will hear five short conversations.
You will hear each conversation twice.
There is one question for each conversation.
For questions 1–5, put a tick ✔ **under the right answer.**

EXAMPLE

0 What time is it?

06.00   07.00   09.00

A ☐   B ☐   C ✔

---

1 Where is Mark going at the weekend?

A ☐   B ☐   C ☐

2 How many students are there at the school?

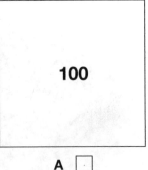   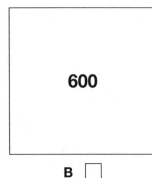   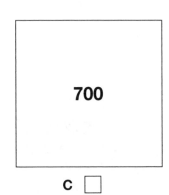

100   600   700

A ☐   B ☐   C ☐

3   Where is the hospital?

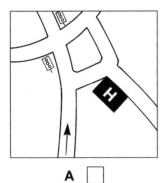

A

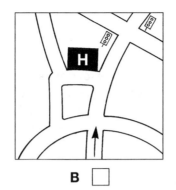

B

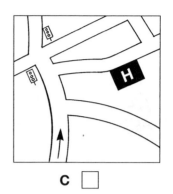

C

4   What must they remember to take?

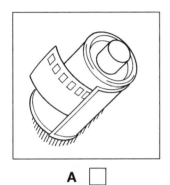

A

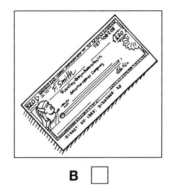

B

C

5   Which is Christina's family?

A

B

C

[Turn over

Part 2

Questions 6 – 10

Tip! *You will hear the people in the same order as the questions.*
If you miss something, don't worry – you will hear everything a second time.
Choose your answers when you listen the first time.
Check your answers when you listen the second time.

Listen to Mario talking to Francesca about his birthday presents.
What presents did each person give Mario?

For questions 6 – 10, write a letter A – H next to each present.
You will hear the conversation twice.

EXAMPLE
0   Dinos   [F]

PEOPLE		PRESENTS
6 Paul ☐		**A** bag
7 Mario's parents ☐		**B** Walkman
8 Mario's sister ☐		**C** computer book
9 Uncle Terry ☐		**D** socks
10 Francesca ☐		**E** summer holiday
		F sweater
		G T-shirt
		H watch

Part 3

Questions 11–15

 Tip! After you hear the instructions, you have twenty seconds to read the questions. Make sure you read them carefully. They will tell you what to listen for.

Listen to Stephanie talking to an assistant at the chemist's about her photographs.
For questions 11–15, tick ✔ A, B or C.
You will hear the conversation twice.

EXAMPLE			
0 Stephanie left her films at the chemist's last	**A**	Monday.	✔
	B	week.	☐
	C	month.	☐

11 Stephanie's ticket is	**A**	broken.	☐
	B	lost.	☐
	C	new.	☐
12 Her surname is	**A**	Philips.	☐
	B	Filipus.	☐
	C	Filips.	☐
13 Some photos are	**A**	very bad.	☐
	B	very dark.	☐
	C	very sunny.	☐
14 Stephanie took some photos from	**A**	too near.	☐
	B	too far away.	☐
	C	the river.	☐
15 The photos cost	**A**	£19.99.	☐
	B	£9.19.	☐
	C	£9.99.	☐

[Turn over

Part 4
Questions 16 – 20

You only need to write one or two words.
Try to write your answers the first time you hear the information.
Check your answers when you listen the second time.
Check your spelling.

You will hear a student telephoning about a weekend job.

Listen and complete questions 16 – 20.
You will hear the conversation twice.

WEEKEND JOB

At:	**16**	Lo-Price
To work:		downstairs
Money (under 18):	**17**	£ per hour
Meet:	**18**	Mrs
Time:	**19**	
Next to:	**20**	

Part 5

Questions 21 – 25

Tip! ≫ *Read the form carefully. Think about the type of answers you need to write. What kind of information is missing?*
Write your answers when you listen the first time. You only need to write one or two words.
Check your answers when you listen the second time.
Check your spelling.

You will hear some information about buses to London.

Listen and complete questions 21 – 25.
You will hear the information twice.

YELLOW BUSES TO LONDON

Monday – Saturday office opens at:	21	
Number of buses to London:	22	each day
Buy tickets from:	23	or on the bus
Student return ticket costs:	24 £	
For sale on bus:	25	and drink

You now have eight minutes to write your answers on the answer sheet.

PAPER 3   Speaking   (8 – 10 minutes)

Following greeting and introductions, the examiner asks each candidate questions.

Each candidate should be able to:

■ talk about where he/she comes from and what he/she does (job or studies).

■ answer general personal questions, e.g. about family, friends.

■ answer questions about their daily life, interests and likes.

Tip! >> *If you don't understand something, ask the examiner to repeat the question! Try to say something more than just 'Yes' or 'No'.*

Answer these questions

1   How do you spell your surname?
2   What subjects do you like at school?
3   Where did you go last weekend?
4   What do you do in your spare time?
5   Which country would you like to visit? Why?
6   Tell me about your family.
7   Tell me about your home town.

Part 2 – prompt card activity (3 – 4 minutes)

In this part the candidates ask each other questions. The questions may be of a personal kind.

The examiner will give Candidate A a prompt card.

Candidate A should ask questions using the words and pictures.

Candidate B should answer using his/her personal experience.

The examiner will stop the conversation after about 4 or 5 questions.

He/She then gives Candidate B a similar prompt card to ask Candidate A questions.

 Tip! >> *There is no 'right question'. It is possible to make more than one question from each prompt.*

Part 2

Candidate A

A, ask **B** some questions about **a book he/she has read**. Use the words and pictures on the card to help you. Ask five questions. **B**, answer **A**'s questions.

A BOOK

Ask your partner questions about a book he/she has read.

name?

long / short?

what kind?

who / about?

why / like?

Candidate B

B, ask **A** some questions about **his/her favourite room**. Use the words and pictures
on the card to help you. Ask five questions. **A**, answer **B**'s questions.

FAVOURITE ROOM

Ask your partner questions about a room he/she likes.

which room?

big / small?

do there?

see outside?

colour?

TEST 4

PAPER 1   Reading and Writing   (1 hour 10 minutes)

Part 1

Questions 1–5

Who are these notices for?
For questions 1–5, mark A, B or C on the answer sheet.

EXAMPLE			ANSWER
0	**Free juice with every pizza!**	A people in a bank B people in a café C people in a museum	B

1 **Left luggage office open 24 hours**

A passengers
B receptionists
C drivers

2 **LOW PRICES ALL WEEK FOR SHIRTS & SKIRTS**

A people selling clothes
B people washing clothes
C people buying clothes

3 *SPECIAL TODAY – omelette and chips! Children half price!*

A people in a restaurant
B people in a supermarket
C people in a zoo

4 **LOOK BOTH WAYS!**

A people at a theatre
B people crossing a road
C people in a bus

5 **BREAKFAST 7–9.30 a.m.**

A hotel guests
B shoppers
C waiters

[Turn over

Questions 6 – 10

Which notice (A – H) says this (6 – 10)?
For questions 6 – 10, mark the correct letter A – H on the answer sheet.

EXAMPLE	ANSWER
0 We are only open in the afternoons.	**F**

6 You must not speak to anyone here.

7 You can stay the night here.

8 You can't leave your car here.

9 You can begin studying soon.

10 You don't have to pay to go in.

A
Parking for buses only

B
No talking in the library please

C
Sports centre – now open all day!

D
GUEST HOUSE
Rooms available

E
No tickets left for tonight's film

F
Museum open 1–6 p.m.

G
French classes start next week

H
CASTLE GARDENS
Entrance free

Part 2

Questions 11 – 15

Read the descriptions (11 – 15) of things you can find in a house.
What is the name (A – H) for each description?
For questions 11 – 15, mark the correct letter A – H on the answer sheet.

EXAMPLE	ANSWER
0 You put your head on this when you sleep.	**E**

11 Two people can speak to each other with this.

12 People sit round this to eat their meals.

13 You put food in this.

14 You sit in this to wash yourself.

15 You use this if you want to drink something.

A bath

B bed

C bowl

D glass

E pillow

F sofa

G table

H telephone

[Turn over

Part 3

Questions 16 – 20

Complete the five conversations.
For questions 16 – 20, mark A, B or C on the answer sheet.

EXAMPLE		ANSWER
0	Where do you come from? **A** France. **B** School. **C** Home.	**A**

16 Can I open the window, please?

     A Yes, it's hot, isn't it?

     B No, it's closed.

     C Where are you going?

17 I went to the bank this morning.

     A Where did you go?

     B I'm afraid not.

     C Oh good, we need some cash.

18 How far is it now?

     A Two months, I think.

     B About five kilometres.

     C It's quite tall.

19 Where are your parents?

     A Fine, thanks.

     B Giovanni and Maria.

     C In Spain.

20 What's the price of that shirt?

     A It's too big.

     B I don't know.

     C Red and white.

Questions 21 – 25

Complete the conversation.
What does Sally say to the receptionist at the Youth Hostel?
For questions 21 – 25, mark the correct letter A – H on the answer sheet.

EXAMPLE	ANSWER
Receptionist: Good afternoon. How can I help you?	
Sally: 0	E

Receptionist: Certainly. For how many people?

Sally: 21 ....

Receptionist: Would you like two double rooms or a large room for four?

Sally: 22 ....

Receptionist: That's fine. How long are you going to stay for?

Sally: 23 ....

Receptionist: And are you members of the Youth Hostel Association?

Sally: 24 ....

Receptionist: OK, can I have your members' cards, please?

Sally: 25 ....

Receptionist: Thank you very much.

A I think we'd rather be in the same room, please.

B We need the room for three nights.

C Of course, here you are.

D Thank you very much for your help.

E I'd like to book a room.

F Do you want me to pay?

G Yes, we are.

H There are four of us in our group.

[Turn over

Part 4

Read the article about shopping in Britain.
Are sentences 26 – 32 'Right' (A) or 'Wrong' (B)?

If there is not enough information to answer 'Right' (A) or 'Wrong' (B), choose 'Doesn't say' (C).

For questions 26 – 32, mark A, B or C on the answer sheet.

SHOPPING HOURS in BRITAIN

Shopping hours in Britain are changing. Until a few years ago, shops opened at nine o'clock in the morning and closed at half past five or six o'clock in the evening. Some also closed for an hour for lunch. In many towns, shops were closed on Wednesday afternoons. On Sundays, nothing was open. But now some shops are open longer hours. Some big shops and many supermarkets never close! If you need a litre of milk or some bread at midnight, you can easily buy it.

For people who work long hours or people who often work at night or early in the morning, like doctors, the new shopping hours are good. If someone finishes work at five o'clock in the morning, they can go to the supermarket on their way home and buy some breakfast or a newspaper or anything else they may need.

But not everyone thinks the new shopping hours are a good thing. Some people say that Sunday is a holiday – who wants to work in a supermarket on a Sunday? But shops are very busy at the weekend and longer shopping hours are here to stay.

0   In the past, shopping hours were different.

    A   Right   **B**   Wrong   **C**   Doesn't say   **A**

26   In the past, some shops closed at lunchtime.

    A   Right   **B**   Wrong   **C**   Doesn't say

27   A few years ago, shops also closed on Saturday afternoons.

    A   Right   **B**   Wrong   **C**   Doesn't say

28   Today, all shops are open for longer hours.

    A   Right   **B**   Wrong   **C**   Doesn't say

29   It's easy to buy food in the middle of the night.

    A   Right   **B**   Wrong   **C**   Doesn't say

30   Doctors buy their breakfast at the supermarket.

    A   Right   **B**   Wrong   **C**   Doesn't say

31   Everyone likes longer shopping hours.

    A   Right   **B**   Wrong   **C**   Doesn't say

32   Sunday shopping is here to stay.

    A   Right   **B**   Wrong   **C**   Doesn't say

[Turn over

Part 5

Questions 33 – 40

Read the article about the world getting hotter.
Choose the best word (A, B or C) for each space (33 – 40).
For questions 33 – 40, mark A, B or C on the answer sheet.

THE WORLD IS GETTING HOTTER

(Adapted from 'Global Warming' published in *Crown* 6th May/June 2001 page 17 © Mary Glasgow Magazines/Scholastic.)

The world is getting hotter because ___0___ us! Our factories, cars, trains and planes ___33___ the air dirty. When ___34___ sun shines, everything gets hot and the dirt stops the hot air from going ___35___ to the sky. Because the hot air has nowhere to go, ___36___ gets hotter.

Already our world is ___37___ than it was one hundred years ago. Hot countries may become drier and the people who live there will not be able to grow enough food. Ice in cold areas ___38___ changing to water because of higher temperatures. When this happens, the seas become bigger. Some towns ___39___ the sea may have a problem soon.

We can help ___40___ we stop making the air dirty but we must do something fast!

EXAMPLE			ANSWER
0 A by	**B** for	**C** of	**C**

33 A make	**B** making	**C** makes
34 A a	**B** the	**C** an
35 A on	**B** at	**C** up
36 A everything	**B** all	**C** every
37 A warm	**B** warmer	**C** warmest
38 A are	**B** be	**C** is
39 A near	**B** to	**C** in
40 A so	**B** if	**C** but

Part 6

Questions 41 – 50

Complete the notes.
Write ONE word in each space (41 – 50).
For questions 41 – 50, write your words on the answer sheet.

Dear Miss Thompson,

I (**Example:** ___am___) sorry, but John can't come ___41___ school
today. He ___42___ got a bad stomachache and he must ___43___
to the doctor. I hope ___44___ will be back at school tomorrow.
Please ask his friend Paul to ___45___ John's homework to him.

Yours sincerely,

Clare Smith (John's mother)

Dear Mrs Smith,

I am sorry John is ___46___ . Paul ___47___ come to your house
after school today. I will give ___48___ all the homework ___49___
John. I hope John feels ___50___ soon.

Yours sincerely,

Mary Thompson (John's teacher)

[Turn over

Part 7

Questions 51 – 55

Read the information about a family who want to book a holiday.
Fill in the information on the Holiday Booking Form for the family.
For questions 51 – 55, write the information on the answer sheet.

Mr Bradbury wants to book a holiday in December. His wife and their daughter (age 10) are going with him. They want to leave on 20th December and have a week in a hotel in London. They must be back home on 27th. They don't want to spend more than one thousand five hundred pounds.

HOLIDAY BOOKING FORM

Surname: 51

Number of adults: 52

Number of children: 53

Travel to: 54

Dates: 20th – 27th December

Maximum price: 55 £

Part 8

Question 56

Read this note from your friend Roberto.

I really need my new CD player back! Why have you still got it?

When can you return it to me? Do you want to borrow it again next week?

Roberto

Write a note to Roberto. Answer his questions.
Write 20 – 25 words.
Write your note on the back of the answer sheet.

PAPER 2 Listening (approximately 25 minutes)

Part 1

Questions 1 – 5

Listen to the tape.
You will hear five short conversations.
You will hear each conversation twice.
There is one question for each conversation.
For questions 1 – 5, put a tick ✔ under the right answer.

EXAMPLE

0 How many people were at the meeting?

3	13	30
A ☐	B ☐	C ✔

---

1 How much was the restaurant bill?

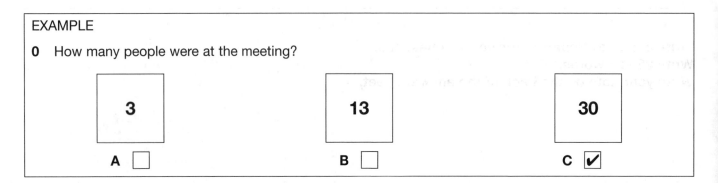

£15	£25	£50
A ☐	B ☐	C ☐

2 How long was the journey?

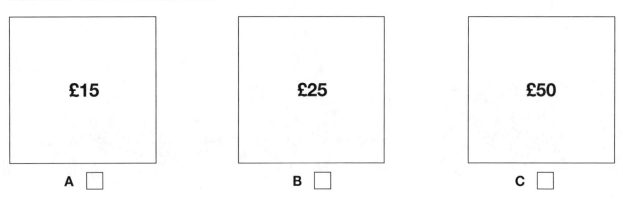

6 hours	10 hours	16 hours
A ☐	B ☐	C ☐

3 What did the man do last night?

A ☐

B ☐

C ☐

4 How does Stefano usually get to school?

A ☐

B ☐

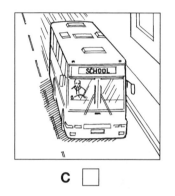

C ☐

5 How did she hear about the accident?

A ☐

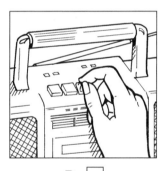

B ☐

C ☐

[Turn over

Part 2

Questions 6 – 10

Listen to David talking to Isabel about his family.
Where did each person go on Saturday?

For questions 6 – 10, write a letter A – H next to each person.
You will hear the conversation twice.

EXAMPLE	
0 Emily	C

6	David's father	☐	
7	Sara	☐	
8	Rob	☐	
9	Ricky	☐	
10	David's mother	☐	

A basketball game

B cinema

C dentist

D restaurant

E shops

F supermarket

G swimming

H tennis lesson

Part 3

Questions 11 – 15

Listen to Anna talking to her friend Sarah about a summer job.
For questions 11 – 15, tick ✔ A, B or C.
You will hear the conversation twice.

EXAMPLE			
0 Sarah's dad needs another	**A**	secretary.	☐
	B	assistant.	✔
	C	manager.	☐

11 Sarah starts work at

- **A** 7.30. ☐
- **B** 8.00. ☐
- **C** 8.30. ☐

12 How much does Sarah earn?

- **A** £4.00 per hour. ☐
- **B** £5.00 per hour. ☐
- **C** £4.50 per hour. ☐

13 For lunch, Sarah usually eats

- **A** pizza. ☐
- **B** sandwiches. ☐
- **C** nothing. ☐

14 Sarah usually eats her lunch

- **A** at Pizza Roma. ☐
- **B** at home. ☐
- **C** in a park. ☐

15 The shop is in

- **A** Byronos Avenue. ☐
- **B** Pyronos Avenue. ☐
- **C** Bironus Avenue. ☐

[Turn over

Part 4

Questions 16 – 20

You will hear a student telephoning a school.

Listen and complete questions 16 – 20.
You will hear the conversation twice.

CROWN ENGLISH LANGUAGE SCHOOL

Next course begins:

Day:	**16**	
Date:	**17**	4th
Classes usually begin at:	**18**	
Address:	**19**	Bridge Road
Next to:	**20**	station

Part 5

Questions 21 – 25

You will hear some information about music classes.

Listen and complete questions 21 – 25.
You will hear the information twice.

$$\equiv \equiv \textit{MUSIC CLASSES} \equiv \equiv$$

PIANO CLASSES:

Days:	**21**	and Thursday or Tuesday and Friday

Classes for:	**22**	hour

Classes cost: £60 per month

GUITAR CLASSES:

Adults pay:	**23** £	per class

Classes start again on:	**24** Monday 23rd

New telephone number:	**25**

You now have eight minutes to write your answers on the answer sheet.

PAPER 3   Speaking   (8 – 10 minutes)

Following greeting and introductions, the examiner asks each candidate questions.

Each candidate should be able to:
- talk about where he/she comes from and what he/she does (job or studies).
- answer general personal questions, e.g. about family, friends.
- answer questions about their daily life, interests and likes.

Answer these questions

1 Have you been to other towns in (your country)?
2 Which school subjects are the most difficult?
3 How do you travel to school each day?
4 Where are you going on holiday this/next year?
5 Tell me something about your home town.
6 Tell me something about your house or flat.

Part 2 – prompt card activity (3 – 4 minutes)

In this part, the candidates ask each other questions. The questions may be of a non-personal kind, e.g. information about a museum.

The examiner will give Candidate A some information and Candidate B some question prompts.

Candidate B should ask the questions and Candidate A should answer them using the information.

The examiner will stop the conversation after about 4 or 5 questions.

He/She then gives the candidates a different set of prompt cards.

Part 2

Candidate A

A, here is some information about **a football game**. (Turn to page 125.)

B, you don't know anything about **the football game** so ask **A** some questions about it. Now, **B**, ask **A** your questions about **the football game** and **A**, you answer them.

Candidate B – your questions

FOOTBALL GAME

- ♦ where?

- ♦ date?

- ♦ time / start?

- ♦ how much?

- ♦ bus?

Candidate B

B, here is some information about **Dino's Snacks**. (Turn to page 127.)

A, you don't know anything about **Dino's Snacks** so ask B some questions about it. Now, A, ask B your questions about **Dino's Snacks** and B, you answer them.

Candidate A – your questions

DINO'S SNACKS

♦ where?

♦ what / food?

♦ open / Saturday?

♦ time / close?

♦ cost / juice?

Extra practice

The extra practice exercises on pages 122 – 127 give you the opportunity to revise some of the language you have practised in this book.

Exercises 1 – 3 help you to revise key vocabulary areas.

Exercises 4 – 7 help you to revise important grammar items:

- prepositions
- word order in sentences and questions
- conjunctions

Exercise 8 helps you to revise punctuation for writing tasks in the exam.

1 〉 *Vocabulary and spelling focus:* anagrams

a 〉 *Rearrange the letters to make the names of things you can read.*

1 Read the .... to find out when the shop opens.   ECOTIN

2 A .... usually has lots of cartoons in it.   IMCOC

3 You need to look at a .... to find out when the train arrives.   BMETLEATI

4 I've got a .... from my parents, who are on holiday in Japan.   ODRPASCT

5 Every month I get a .... about my favourite sport: basketball.   NAGMIEZA

6 My father reads the .... every day.   EPSWENPRA

b 〉 *Rearrange the letters to make the names of jobs.*

1 A .... takes pictures.   RHRGOTEHPOPA

2 My father is a .... He makes bread and cakes.   KEABR

3 Last week my sister's car broke down and she took it to the ....   CEHMNCAI

4 Stefanie is a .... in a hotel – she answers the phone and helps the guests.   TESTECPINRIO

5 You go to a .... if you do not feel very well.   RTOCOD

6 A lot of .... come to our town in summer.   USTORSTI

7 My brother wants to be a .... when he grows up.   IOLPT

8 You can book your holiday at the ....   EVLTAR G'SATNE

··

TEST 2

Paper 3, Speaking Part 2   page 79

Candidate A – your answers

2 〉 *Vocabulary focus:* word sets

a 〉 *Put the words in the box into the right group below.*

classroom ~~passport~~ zoo desk planet suitcase earth guest
tour guide journey lesson ticket library rain forest museum
plants scientist computer teacher homework sunshine

GROUP	WORDS		
People and things to do with holidays (7 words)	...passport...	....	....
	....	....	....
	....		
People and things to do with school (7 words)	....	....	....
	....	....	....
	....		
People and things to do with the natural world (7 words)	....	....	....
	....	....	....
	....		

b 〉 *Complete each sentence with a word from the table above. Use the correct form,
singular or plural.*

Holidays

1 There were more than 250 .... staying in our hotel.

2 Marios packed all his clothes in his ....

3 We bought our .... at the travel agent's.

4 The train .... from our town to the mountains was very long.

School

1 I usually do my .... in my bedroom.

2 I often borrow books from the school ....

3 Every student in my school has his or her own ....

4 My .... is large and the walls are painted white.

Natural world

1 There are many different types of animal in our local ....

2 Some of the trees in the .... are over 50 metres high!

3 We grow .... and flowers in our garden.

4 My mother is a .... She studies the environment.

3 ⟩ Vocabulary focus: crossword puzzle

a⟩ Read the clues and fill in the spaces. All the words are taken from Tests 1–4. Make up your own clue for SUPERMARKET!

1 Someone who travels on a train, bus or plane, but doesn't drive it. (9 letters)

2 This word describes some wild animals. It means the opposite of *safe*. (9)

3 Watch straps are sometimes made of this. (7)

4 You have this when you catch a cold or flu. (11)

5 A shape with four sides. (6)

6 A lot of people in Britain like to put this on toast or bread. (9)

7 You wear this in the winter to keep you warm. (7)

8 The day before Friday. (8)

9 The first meal of the day. (9)

10 You can see plays here. (7)

11 A very useful book when you don't know the meaning of a word. (10)

12 .... (11)

b⟩ Put the words from Exercise a⟩ into the correct groups. Two words don't belong to any group. Then add three more words to each group.

People	Days of the week	Food and meals	Shapes and materials	Clothes	Health	Places
....	....	....	....	....	....	....
....	....	....	....	....	....	....
....	....	....	....	....	....	....
....	....	....	....	....	....	....
		....	....			....

4 〉 *Grammar focus:* prepositions (free time)

Fill in the spaces with the correct preposition: at, in, on, to.

1 A: Where are you going?

   B: I'm going .... the cinema with Julia.

2 A: What time does the concert start?

   B: I think it begins .... nine o'clock.

3 A: When shall we go to the beach?

   B: Let's go .... Saturday.

4 A: I usually get up at six .... the morning.

   B: Really? That's very early!

5 A: Where's Ines?

   B: She's .... the theatre.

6 A: When are you going to play football?

   B: .... Saturday afternoon.

7 A: What shall we do .... the weekend?

   B: I'd like to visit the museum.

8 A: I'm going shopping .... the morning.

   B: Can I come with you?

9 A: Would you like to come .... the match with me?

   B: Yes, what time does it start?

10 A: When's your birthday?

    B: It's .... 19th October.

5 〉 *Grammar focus:* prepositions (travel and transport)

a 〉 *Fill in the spaces with the correct preposition: by, from, in, on, to.*

1 I go .... school .... bus every day.

2 I enjoy travelling .... train.

3 Our neighbours went .... France last year.

4 I've never been .... China, but I would like to go.

5 I like to spend the holidays .... the mountains.

6 My best friend was .... Spain .... holiday last month.

7 My family stayed .... a big hotel near the sea last summer.

8 It isn't far .... my house to the beach.

b 〉 *Read the sentences in Exercise* a 〉 *again. Are they true (✔) or false (✘) for you?*

....

TEST 4

Paper 3, Speaking Part 2   page 119

Candidate A – your answers

Saturday 29th November

FOOTBALL GAME

Bridge End School and Howard's School

Game starts 4.00 p.m.

FREE ADMISSION!

Oxford Football Field
(Get bus number 47)

For more information: Tel 8678 1543

6 > *Grammar focus:* word order

> *Put the words into the correct order to make sentences or questions.*

1 school / My / called / is / St John's

....

2 have / two / I / sisters / and / brother / one

....

3 do / you / What / usually / at / do / weekends

.... ?

4 favourite / is / hamburger and chips / My / food

....

5 holiday / on / year / Where / you / did / last / go

.... ?

6 do / books / best / What kind of / you / like

.... ?

7 > *Grammar focus:* conjunctions

a > <u>Underline</u> *the correct conjunction in each sentence.*

1 I wanted to play football *and/but/or* it was raining.
2 We like animals *so/because/but* we are going to get a dog.
3 Gina didn't go out *so/because/and* she had to do her homework.
4 We went to see the castle *or/but/and* then we went to a museum.
5 Tomorrow we could play football *because/or/but* go to the cinema.
6 It's my birthday on Saturday *so/because/but* I'm having a party.

TEST 2

Paper 3, Speaking Part 2   page 79

Candidate B – your answers

b) *Read the letter from Mark to Lisa. Complete the spaces with the correct conjunction from the box below.*

and	or	so
because	but	

Dear Lisa,

Thanks for your note. I haven't phoned you .... I haven't been very well. Last week I had to go to the doctor .... he told me not to go to school for three .... four days. I think I will be back on Monday next week .... I'm not sure yet. Chris sent me an email with the homework .... I have plenty of things to do here at home. I won't get bored!

See you soon.

Mark

8 ⟩ *Skills focus:* punctuation

, a comma	' an apostrophe	. a full stop	? a question mark	CAPITAL LETTERS

a) *Add capital letters, commas and full stops to the sentences.*

1 ryan giggs the famous manchester united footballer was born in 1973
2 the first team he played for was manchester city
3 giggs also plays for his country wales
4 he first played for wales when he was only 17 years old
5 giggs has also been the captain of the welsh team
6 he likes swimming hang gliding and reading

b) *Read the note opposite and add the correct punctuation in the spaces: two full stops, three question marks and two apostrophes. You also need to add five capital letters.*

Dear john,

we ..... ll be in Bournemouth tomorrow at six o'oclock ..... can we meet you ..... what time will you be free ..... shall we bring our swimming things with us ..... I ..... ll call you when we arrive ....

Peter and Lisa

TEST 4

Paper 3, Speaking Part 2   page 120

Candidate B – your answers

DINO'S SNACKS

89 CAMBRIDGE ROAD

TAKE AWAY OR EAT IN

MONDAY – SATURDAY
6.00 a.m. – midnight

NO SMOKING!

Sandwiches from £1.50   Pizzas from £3.50   Juices 90p

Pearson Education Limited
Edinburgh Gate
Harlow
Essex CM20 2JE
England
And Associated Companies throughout the World.

www.longman.com

ISBN 0 582 77358 X

Set in 10.25pt Helvetica 55 Roman, 10.25pt Stone Serif

Printed in Spain by Graficas Estella

First published 2002

Publisher's acknowledgements

We are grateful to Mary Glasgow Magazines for permission to
reproduce extracts adapted from 'Global Warming' published in *Crown*
6th May/June 2001 page 17 © Mary Glasgow Magazines/Scholastic,
and 'Beverly Hills High' published in *Crown* 1st September/October
2001 pages 10 – 11 © Mary Glasgow Magazines/Scholastic.

We are indebted to the University of Cambridge Local Examinations
Syndicate (UCLES) for permission to reproduce UCLES material.

Author's acknowledgements

Many thanks to all the teachers at Forum Language Centre, Nicosia,
Cyprus, for their help, encouragement and support during the writing
of this book: Vincent Allen, Derek Bickerstaffe, Maria Christou, Costas
Djapouras, Anthos Ladomatos, Stavroulla Marangou, Dora Shiakallis,
Katerina Yiacoumis.

Dedication

For Lydia, Sara & Emily

Illustrations by Gary Rees and Pavely Arts
Designed by Michael Harris